IN OUR OWN WORDS

The First 40 Years
of the Morrisville College
Journalism Program

Compiled and edited by Nancy Cardillo,
Frank Eltman, and Jim Johnson

LOG CABIN BOOKS

Log Cabin Books, 6607 Craine Lake Road, Hamilton, NY 13346

Visit our website at www.logcabinbooks.us

Printed in the United States of America
First printing: December 2007

Library of Congress Cataloging-in-Publication No. 2007938287
In Our Own Words: The First 40 Years of the Morrisville College
Journalism Program / Nancy Cardillo, Frank Eltman, Jim Johnson

ISBN 978-0-9755548-3-8

All profits from the sale of this book benefit the
Journalism Department at Morrisville State College.

DEDICATION

For 40 years, the Morrisville College Journalism Department in central New York has set the standard for producing college students who excel in reporting, editing, photography, publicity, and broadcasting. This book is dedicated to all those wonderful professors who had the vision to establish the program, and to those who maintain that standard today.

Newswriting Class in 1976

Contents

Foreword

The year 2007 marks the 40th anniversary of the Journalism Program on the SUNY Morrisville campus. During that period more than 1,500 students have been graduated and taken their places in various communications media. Large numbers have distinguished themselves with prestigious honors and awards.

Four publishers planted the seeds of the idea that grew into a two-year journalism program at SUNY Morrisville. The program was designed to prepare reporters and photographers for positions at small daily and weekly papers. No one ever dreamed of the heights to which our graduates would soar.

Mario Rossi of the Syracuse Post Standard, Mike Milmoe of the Canastota Bee Journal, John Tuttle of the Oneida Dispatch and Mason Taylor of the Utica Daily Press could not have envisioned a Pulitzer Prize and three Pulitzer nominations.

The great success this program has enjoyed over its history can be largely attributed to a sense of "family" that has prevailed throughout the years. The close relationship between the J-faculty and its students has been the marvel of the entire campus community. The faculty's open-door policy at all times allowed students to get extra help, air their problems to a sympathetic ear, or just simply have someone to talk to.

To this day I still have several hundred alumni with whom I am in contact. On a fairly regular basis I get e-mails letting me know where they are, how they're doing, and just how much their two years at Mo'ville meant to them.

Finally, I would like to acknowledge those who were most helpful to me in making this program as great as it is. Thanks to Neal Bandlow, Mary Ellen Mengucci, President Royson Whipple, Vice President John Stewart, Dan Reeder, Charlie Hammond, Joe Quinn, Jay Kaplowitz and, finally but especially, my wife, Barbara.

Quoting the words of Paul Harvey, my favorite radio journalist, here's "the rest of the story."

Jerry Leone, Journalism Chair
1967 - 1995

Preface

Nancy Cardillo (Class of '77) was the first among us to receive notice of the college's plan to recognize the 40th anniversary of the school's journalism program. She emailed Frank Eltman ('78) and me with a suggestion to offer a tribute to the program's original mainstays: "Wouldn't it be great if we created a little journal from the alumni to present to Jerry (Leone) and Neal (Bandlow) at the reunion?"

A few short replies later, the idea was expanded and it was posited that we solicit contributions from all our fellow grads and truly "write the book" on the best 2-year journalism program in the country.

The word went out electronically and in direct mail, with a relatively simple assignment presented to each alumnus. Give us 500 words (of course, adhering to all AP Style Book standards) on any of the topics anchoring each section of this collection.

The responses tell a story about a high school teacher, the son of a renowned journalist, who took a leap of faith 40 years ago and initiated what would become a revered journalism program in a central New York county that boasted more cows than people in its census.

It's the story of how he recruited some of the finest teaching talent in the country to take that leap with him and mold fresh groups of mostly teenagers—every two years!—to become some of the finest communicators in their profession.

It's a commentary on how just two short years in a nurturing environment can have a lifelong impact on the students in the program. Most of the alumni have never met, yet we share the same passion and motivation to be precise and concise and to get the story right because of our instructors. It's a story about all that is good with New York's state university system.

As one graduate put it, "I got my job because of my master's degree. But what I *do* every day, I learned at Morrisville."

- Jim Johnson ('78)

Jerry Leone in 1976
—Photo by Barbara Strollo Wetmore

SECTION 1

In the Beginning, We Had Saddle Shoes

1

Earn Upwards of $4,200 a Year
By Joe Sutherland
Class of 1969

Obvious . . .

It's obvious to everyone who went through those first two years of the journalism program at Morrisville what Jerry Leone meant to us, and what he still means to us. He was our big brother. He was the man we all wanted to please . . . he was the teacher we all didn't want to let down.

He had that voice . . . that "everything is going to be ok" type of voice. All of my good memories of Morrisville either begin with, or come back to Jerry.

Now that the obvious is out of the way, let me share some memories of those first days and months and the first two years of the program. A walk down memory lane, better known as Route 20:

The first recollection of Morrisville was at orientation in May of 1967 in Hamilton Hall. My dad and I drove north that morning from my hometown in the Hudson Valley. I had never been more than 50 miles from home. After remarks by President Royson Whipple, the accepted journalism students were directed to the Library Classroom Building. Jerry Leone was still teaching at Tonawanda High School and had no idea what was happening 200 miles to the east. As one of the college deans talked about the program, he uttered a great line that I would hear again in a future movie, "Broadcast News". His remark went something like this: "I see no reason why graduates can't go out to newspapers, radio stations and television stations in Central New York . . . and earn upwards of $4,200 a year." My father and I looked at each other, and my dad said: "Not bad!"

The next memory is one that many of us will take with us throughout our lives. . . it's the first time we met Jerry. I believe it was Bicknell Hall, first floor . . . first meeting of the first class. It seems we were all there early. Everybody was nervous. But it was a good nervous . . . like the anticipation of prom night, or driving to NYC and seeing Yankee Stadium for the first time, thinking you'll never get in before the first pitch. Then Jerry walked in. It was Monday, September 11, 1967. He was more nervous than we were and shaking from his head right down to his scruffy saddle shoes. Fifty minutes later, the first class ended . . . and our lives were changed forever.

A million wonderful things happened during the next 21 months before graduation – a few bad things happened too. Dr. King and Bobby Kennedy were killed in 1968 . . . Jerry was injured in a freak accident that summer . . . my roommate's brother-in-law died in Vietnam in October of '68 . . . but mostly, every day at Morrisville was a good day when Jerry was part of the equation.

My final memory is graduation day, June 7, 1969. Jerry was saying his farewells in East Hall. We shook hands. He didn't say a word and neither did I.

It's obvious what I felt at that moment.

Obvious.

Joe brings more than 35 years of experience -- in public relations, on Capitol Hill and in newspaper reporting -- to Burness Communications. Since joining the company in 1993, Joe has specialized in media relations. He has served a broad range of clients, including the Pew Initiative on Food and Biotechnology, Jack Kent Cooke Foundation, National Science & Technology Medals Foundation, the Howard Hughes Medical Institute, the National Bioethics Advisory Commission, and the International Maize and Wheat Improvement Center.

A New York native and long-time resident of Washington, Joe graduated from Morrisville State College (NY) and the University of Dayton and has done graduate work at St. John's University and George Washington University. He began his career as a teacher in the public schools in Dayton, Ohio, before working for Gannett Newspapers at locations in New York State. He came to Washington in the mid-70s and served as press secretary to U.S. Rep. Benjamin A. Gilman. From there, Joe worked as a media relations manager at General Dynamics Corp.

He has been married for 33 years to Ann DeStefano Sutherland, a television producer in Washington. They have one son, Stephen, a student at Santa Clara University, and a basset hound, Otis. Joe, forgive him, loves the Yankees and the Dayton Flyers.

2

'Virtual' Photography in 1967?

By Frank Kourt
Class of 1969

As I settled into campus life at Morrisville in the fall of 1967, I found myself anticipating new academic experiences. Photography was high on my list, since I had spent much of my youth behind the viewfinders of Brownies and Instamatics, and wanted to learn how the pros did it. The long-awaited photography class finally rolled around, and I showed up, proudly toting the second-hand range finder 35 mm camera I had purchased for the class.

There was only one problem. Jerry Leone, sole journalism instructor and founder of the journalism program, informed us that film had not yet arrived. Slightly flustered, but undaunted, Jerry directed us to spend the session using our empty cameras to *pretend* to take pictures.

It would, he assured us, teach us "composition." To this day, I reflect on the absurdity of this group of fledgling photographers running around campus, dutifully snapping pictures with empty cameras, at the urging of our instructor who, we were later to find out, was busily teaching HIMSELF some photographic fundamentals so that he could stay one step ahead of us.

Why does this incident stand out in my Morrisville journalism experience? Well, partly, I guess, because over the last 40 years, I have developed an appreciation for the absurd...

But, it's more than that. The incident epitomized the essence of the fledgling journalism program.

For one thing, it underlined the unbridled enthusiasm that we young pioneers had for the program, a kind of *esprit de corps* that said, "no matter what it is---film or no film, we can get it done." I like to think we were a particularly tight group for those two years. After all, we were the oddballs on campus. While practically everyone else was learning a traditional trade; be it electronics or auto mechanics, we were sitting be-

4

hind typewriters and running around campus taking pictures sans film. Another thing about this struck me recently. If it were 40 years later, we probably wouldn't have needed film. We might well have been running around with digital cameras. I'm glad we learned the "old fashioned" way, though. Today I am inordinately proud of the fact that I can look at an overcast day and know that if I have 125 ASA film in my camera, I can get a decent image by shooting one frame at 125 speed, F 5.6 and another at F 8.0. Light meters? We don't need no stinkin' light meters!

That's another part of the essence of the journalism program. It taught us to do everything from taking a pretty good photo to basic layout to writing everything from sports to investigative pieces.

The skills I learned at Morrisville have held me in good stead throughout my career, and still do in semi-retirement.

And, who knows? Maybe taking pictures without film back on that crisp Central New York autumn day so long ago actually did teach us about composition …

Frank Kourt is a semi-retired communications professional, living in Richmond, Kentucky with "the fabulous" Patsy Ann Wheeler. He worked as a reporter-photographer for the Binghamton (NY) Press for nine years, earning a BS in Communications from Empire State College.

He pursued a career in public relations, working for ITT Educational Services, and in public relations management positions for several Chicago-area health care institutions. He is retired from the public relations department of The College of Lake County, Grayslake, Ill. He edits a magazine, "Living Well-50-Plus," and has written freelance pieces for many newspapers and magazines, including "The Richmond Register" and "The Lexington Herald-Leader."

He has a weekly cooking column, "The Food Dude," for "The Week," a newspaper covering Walworth County, Wisconsin. He is accredited in the practice of public relations (APR) by the Public Relations Society of America.

3

How *The Chimes* Got Its Name

By Frank Kourt
Class of 1969

It happened on a cold and snowy day in February, 1969.
SUNY Morrisville was about to get its own newspaper.

The question was, as (my future wife) Cindy Hathaway, Joe Sutherland, Jim Flateau, and Al Lawrence sat around a table with our faculty advisor, Jerry Leone: what would the name for the newspaper be?

We sat… and we thought... brainstorming...

The cold, grey winter oppressed us…. We really didn't want to be there, but, suddenly, the campus chimes rang out the four o'clock hour.

"There it is!" Cindy exclaimed.

"There's what?" we all asked.

"The Chimes," she said.

The chimes on campus in those days rang the hour… just like Big Ben. And it was something we took for granted.

What better name for the newspaper? (She got extra credit!)

The Chimes it was!

I was madly in love with Ms. Hathaway, and already knew I was going to marry that gorgeous 19-year-old woman. We wed in December of that same year, and had nearly 33 years of a wonderful life together.

So, folks, whenever you hear those chimes, and whenever you wonder how that paper got its name, think of a beautiful 19-year-old girl who became my wife, a lady who always smiled and loved life, Cynthia Hathaway Kourt (1949-2002).

That's the way it was, just the way I remember it, and just 40 short years ago! We also ran the radio station, WCVM, back in those days.

I was the Program Director (The Big Cheese). I had a Music Director (Cindy), a News Director (Jim Kenyon, who was succeeded by Jim Flateau), and various sports directors and special events people who made the whole crazy thing a success.

A "pirate" radio station, we were, at the time, technically illegal. If the FCC came calling, we'd all be up on a federal rap. Nobody cared. We just kept broadcasting on our (I think it was, at that time) 5 watts of pure power! When the transmitter went down, I'd say to our resident techie, "Do what you can, Scotty!"

We did "block" programming at that time. (I would do "hard rock" for, say, from 7 to 8 p.m. (HERE'S THE LATEST FROM THE JEFFERSON AIRPLANE), and then switch, with the appropriate mellow voice, to "easy listening" (Sinatra, et al) from 9 to 10. I thought at the time that it didn't sound like the same guy.

Cindy would make the "Top 50 Chart" based, in part, on what the part-time janitor who cleaned up the radio station thought.

It pleases me, in my old age, to look back and see how well we've all done.

It really all goes back to Morrisville. So many successful lives...so many good friends...so many memories!

Anyhow, if you're still with me, that's the honest and true story of how The Chimes got its name. I know; I was there in 1969!

Keep ringing those Chimes!

1969

Today

4

Who Doesn't Love a Byline?

By Jeanne "Tra" Trabold Heller
Class of 1969

In the beginning, there was just Jerry Leone and us; a classroom of eager freshmen excited to begin our college years. What we failed to appreciate at the time, because after all it was all about *us*, was how eager and excited Jerry was as well. He had just "graduated" from teaching high school to become a SUNY Morrisville professor and lucky for us, his enthusiasm and zeal for the Journalism program became contagious. Jerry *was* the program, teaching every single class and there was devotion to this task from both sides.

So in our second year, when The Chimes moved from concept to realty, we editors felt enormously privileged to be involved. As usual, secondhand, cramped space was our domain, but the bathrooms were clean and we loved our special area. We had some deficiencies (layout!) that soon became apparent, but the rings of armpit sweat seemed to diminish each time we successfully met our deadline. Who doesn't love a byline?

Spring came and I had a tip from Jerry about a groundbreaking for a new education building and I planned to follow up. The night before that event, I discovered I had totally forgotten to prepare for a debate at 8 a.m. the next day for a class taught by the magnificent Prof. Taze R. Huntley. This was 1969...no computers, no internet, no late hours at the library, and female students had curfews. There was no way to do research for this debate.

After a sleepless night, I was at the library at its opening only to find that any books relative to my subject were already checked out -- by my opponent. My simple solution was to cut the class and spend the time with pounding heart, feeling nauseous, head down in a study carrel. One miserable, stomach-churning hour later, I realized it would be impossible to hide forever and went to Madison Hall to face Prof. Huntley. I explained respectfully, begged forgiveness, and was offered the opportunity for another debate on another topic—against him. I chose to view this as a victory. For the remainder of that day, everywhere I turned, I bumped into Prof. Huntley. He was in the Quad, in the Student Union, on walkways, and in late afternoon, flexing his knees behind the handle of the silver shovel for the groundbreaking I was covering for The Chimes. We were able to look each other in the eye during that interview, standing on the grassy field while a gentle wind blew from the south, carrying the quintessential Morrisville aroma, *eau de dairy barn*.

So what wisdom have I gleaned in these 40 years since the Journalism program began? First, gravity wins. Okay, this has nothing to do with journalism but it is true. Second, always be honest and respectful of your sources and your readers. Finally, I know to my very core that Jerry likes us best!

Jeanne (Tra') Trabold Heller served as an advertising copywriter for Sibley's Department Store (now closed). She was a freelance advertising copywriter for Mike Verno Advertising (now closed). She also served as an advertising copywriter for Cole Advertising (now closed). She was involved in Corporate/Investor Relations for the Rochester Community Savings Bank (now closed)

Do we see a trend?

She is now working as a paralegal for the Monroe County District Attorney's Office in Economic Crime. Considering the plethora of criminals who believe they really can beat the system, "Tra" feels this position is the one that may actually take her into retirement.

She has been married for 37 years, with three daughters and one adored grandson, and lives in Rochester, New York.

She reports that she enjoyed writing this much more than expected!

5

Journalism Helped Me *Sea* the World

By Ken Cronk
Class of 1969

Late in the fall of 1969, some guy in a shiny suit pulled a piece of paper with the date of my birth on it out of a box. There was no doubt that I would soon be drafted, so I joined the Navy as a preventative. It worked extraordinarily well. Twenty-seven years later, I retired from that great institution and began my second career as a civilian public servant in government public affairs

In a career that took me to Viet Nam, the three coasts of the U.S., two years living in Athens, dozens of four and five day port calls in the Far East, Northern Europe and the Mediterranean, there was one constant. When the people I worked for found out I could make words into sentences, sentences into paragraphs, and paragraphs into reports and correspondence that made sense, my life became easier. That was when and how I discovered the first tangible benefit of my time learning the inverted pyramid, organization, observation, and accuracy. That much, at least, stuck to me from my time at Morrisville with Jerry Leone. There was a lot to learn yet, of course; the learning continues to this day. But the foundation was laid there in Morrisville.

After my first four years, I changed my career field permanently to Navy journalist and began to write, edit and take pictures full time—*schweet*. Twelve years later, I finished my bachelor's degree, applied for a commission as an officer, and became a public affairs officer for the Navy.

The most significant story I ever covered is… I'll be damned if I know. There were some great ones, though. Around 1976, I interviewed a Navy Captain named Grace Hopper in her musty-smelling Pentagon basement office. Captain Hopper was the co-inventor of the COBOL computer language and a pioneer in programming and in introducing printed circuitry and "chips" to Navy leaders who thought the more tubes a computer had and the more it weighed, the better it was.

A cereal bowl overflowing with Lucky Strike butts was on her desk and one smoldered between her fingers. She was lively, irreverent, and filled with revolutionary ideas. I don't recall a single word of the interview, and it was years later when I understood the significance of that encounter. She opened my eyes to change and made me realize the value of looking forward—and the futility of looking back.

Another important interview took place in April 1980. Helicopters were preparing to launch from the deck of the aircraft carrier USS Nimitz in an attempt to rescue U.S. hostages in Iran. I was doing on-camera interviews of members of the team that were to be aired after the attempt. The operation ended in a disaster that took the lives of two of the Marines I interviewed. I never again saw or heard of the film of my interview.

If I or any of my classmates had not gone to Morrisville, would we still have had interesting experiences? I would say certainly. What is special about the experience then, is that it happened to me in the presence of the others who were there. The same goes for them, I suppose. The experience is special because it is ours, and it did have some role in shaping and informing the first, shaky steps of what became, eventually, a career.

Ken followed his associate's degree in Journalism from Morrisville almost 20 years later with a bachelor's degree in Liberal Arts from Excelsior University in 1987 and a masters in Human Resources Development from Webster University.

11

6

Ruminating on 30+ Years

By Karen (Budzynski) Knight
Class of 1975

As I contemplated the 40th anniversary of the Journalism program reunion, I had a flood of memories from my years in the early '70's at Morrisville. Some highlights:

- As editor of *The Chimes*, our editorial mission was to change the campus book store – encouraging its manager to take advantage of our business program experts so the store would meet the needs of "today's" students and customers regarding how it looked, what it sold, and how it operated.
- The advice and counsel Neal, Dan, Charlie and Jerry provided throughout the years. I remember one instance: When I was considered for the editor's role at the "Chittenango-Bridgeport Times," I was offered $200/week salary. Since I was a young college kid who didn't have a clue what it cost to live outside of the Mo'ville campus, I sought the advice of Charlie Hammond, my advisor. He suggested asking for $250/week. My publisher thought he could get someone with experience for that price, and advertised the job opening in "Editor & Publisher." No one responded, and we settled at $225/week. This was 1975...
- Art Pastore.
- Twenty-five-cent beers. Thursday nights. The Shamrock. The pizza and roast beef subs.
- Drinking black coffee at dinner, piling the cups on top of each other to see who could drink the most.
- Covering the arson fires at Helyar Hall. Being frightened by the possibility that it could have been your dorm.
- The closeness of the Journalism class. The closeness of the kids from the Buffalo area. The continued friendship today of the Buffalo crowd.

- Getting together with Dan and Janet Reeder at their house and enjoying brownies. Then getting together with Dan and Janet in Lawrence, Kansas a few years later.
- Tasting lobster for the first time at a luncheon with Royson Whipple, college president. As editor of the Chimes, I was now considered a 'student leader,' and Roy had invited a group of us to lunch to meet.
- Learning that sometimes best friends can't be roommates. And surviving to still be best friends.
- Stopping on the way home in Canandaigua for dinner with my Dad.

As I look back at my short time at Mo'ville, the memories bring warm smiles—of people, of what we learned, and how we prepared for the real world. Certainly the skills I learned helped get me started; even though I "sold my soul" to corporate America, where I still use those skills every day!

To Jerry, Neal, Dan, (and Charlie) – thank you for the vision, and for the tenacity to make it happen. Thank you for sharing your knowledge and wisdom. And finally, thank you to the Class of '75 (and '74) for the memories.

In April 1975, Karen became editor of a small weekly newspaper in Chittenango, NY, about 30 miles from Morrisville in the birthplace of L. Frank Baum, the author of the "Wizard of Oz." As editor of the "Chittenango-Bridgeport Times," she covered the local town and village governments, school boards, schools and their activities, and other happenings in this small community. She was editor, writer, photographer and the graphic layout department, even spending some time "setting type" on the Compugraphic.

The circulation quickly increased by over 25 percent, and during her four-year stint, her efforts were recognized by the National Newspaper Association for best photography and editorial pages. In 1979, she joined IBM in the Communications Department, rose through the ranks, and worked in the various parts of IBM Corporate Communications for the next 27 years. In 2006 she made a career change and joined IBM's consulting group, where she now provides organizational change management, including communications, to customers who have decided to outsource part of their business to IBM. She hopes to retire in 2013.

7

Oneidans are force behind Pulitzer

By David Hollis, Editor
Reprinted from The Oneida Daily Dispatch—February 11, 1983

Pulitzer.

In the newspaper industry, the name is holy.

Up until a recently over-publicized divorce case, the name of this publishing family and the prize it presents was unsullied.

That, however, is not the topic at hand.

What is at hand is local talent, local resources, local assets most people overlook.

We recently carried a story about two SUNY-Morrisville grads nominated for the Pulitzer Prize. Jim Flateau was nominated for some investigative reporting about the Mafia and Joseph Traver was nominated for his photo of the U.S. hockey team winning in the Olympics in Lake Placid.

They don't work here, but the men who trained them and the school they come from are very much a big part of this area.

Jerry Leone, who lives on Birchwood Drive in Oneida, is a pretty normal character... with a few exceptions. These include:

1. He believes that ethics are the basics of newspapering; something that is not always at the front of a lot of people's minds.

2. He loves his job. He believes in teaching and believes in doing it right. He is dedicated to his students and the profession. SUNY-Morrisville may not be aware of the asset it has in this man. The city of Oneida should know it too.

3. He gives students nuts and bolts journalism which will allow them to get jobs. Leone, rightly, skirts all the lofty nonsense about the profession, and teaches his kids the craft. That is rare; most J-profs want to pontificate.

4. He wears saddle shoes.

There's more—not much more, because it's a small program—to SUNY-Morrisville's journalism program than Leone. There's Neal Bandlow. Like Leone, he lives in Oneida (South Street) and is fairly mainstream. In Bandlow, there are special exceptions, such as:

1. In the pit of his stomach burns a fire, a flame that drives him to be better than what he is. Each day is a new chance to do better in this man's eyes and he translates that belief to the students he teaches. That is rare.

2. He, like Leone, is of the mind that as the student twig is bent, so grows the professional tree. He's demanding, but he's no ogre.

3. He wants more... not for himself, but for the program, for the kids. He wants to make things better.

4. He hails from the same home town I do, and has probably forgotten that many years ago as a guest at the Hollis family reunion, he nearly drowned me at Lakeside Park in Port Huron, MI.

These men, and the handful of others in the department are concerned about the state of journalism education, and try their darndest to always make their kids take the high road.

We have some proof of that ourselves. Dispatch Sports Editor Frank Eltman is a product of Morrisville. We're lucky to have him on board and hired him because he had the Leone-Bandlow treatment when he went to school. Too, Mike Gormley, one of our reporters, came from the same school. It won't be long, I trust, before Gormley will be writing for a larger paper and making more money. He was well-prepared for the job and has proven himself here.

Bandlow and Leone had steered us away from grads who weren't the quality of Eltman and Gormley and did so to ensure the integrity of the program. I thank them for that.

SUNY-Morrisville is a small fish swimming in the same sea with places like Missouri University, Columbia, Michigan State and Northwestern. However, it doesn't have to turn tail and swim away. It does what it's supposed to do: prepare kids to get jobs when they graduate. College tuition is an investment, and the journalism program at SUNY-Morrisville would trade well if placed on the stock exchange.

It's limited in many ways. But the hard work of men like Leone and Bandlow and others help give it the reputation of one of the finest two-year journalism programs in the nation.

Think of that for a moment.

Then, think that these guys are your neighbors, and that SUNY-Morrisville is part of your community, too. Think of that. Let it seep in. Let it remind you that there is yet another reason why Madison County and the city of Oneida are great places to be.

Original postscript: David Hollis is the editor of the Oneida Daily Dispatch and never went to journalism school. However, he shares Neal Bandlow's love for the Tigers... even when they finish in the second division. He's even thought of buying saddle shoes.

Updated postscript: David Hollis has worked as a newspaper reporter and editor, public relations executive, and columnist for many years. His latest venture is Radio Free Hamilton, a full-service news Web site serving the Hamilton, NY area. It can be found at http://www.radiofreehamilton.com.

**Award-winning photojournalist Joe Traver ('72) presents a
pair of saddle shoes to Jerry Leone**

8

Still on the Job After 38 Years

By Norm Landis
Class of 1969

When editors and publishers pushed for a program at SUNY Morrisville to train people to be reporters and editors for small and medium-sized papers, I wonder if they thought some of us would stay for our whole careers—with a couple of the first class still going today.

I'm certain they never imagined they could find out what we were up to if they "Googled" us.

In Lyndonville I had done a few things for the school paper, but was not sure what I wanted to become. When it was announced that a representative from Morrisville would be there and the college offered journalism, it sounded interesting. Maybe I could work for National Geographic and be sent around the world.

Also accepted at Brockport, I figured after two years at Morrisville I'd have a degree but if I went to Brockport two years and ran out of money or interest, I wouldn't, so I headed to Morrisville. The tour guides tried to be helpful ("here's a typing room – you'll probably be in here at least part of the time") but it was tough because the program didn't exist.

Near the end of the two years, I borrowed a VW from a local underclassman and went to the Oneida Daily Dispatch for an interview, agreeing to start work the Monday after graduation – possibly making me the first grad on the job. I was sports editor of a daily newspaper at age 20! Besides the local gal Debby Austin on the LPGA tour, I met Carol Mann, visited world welterweight boxing champ Billy Backus in his home, met his uncle Carmen Basilio (welter and middleweight champ), other boxers and covered another boxer speaking at Colgate -- one Cassius Clay. A Baseball Hall of Fame official praised my photo of an induction and I covered area drivers at Watkins Glen.

I was switched over to news and putting in long hours. I talked to a photographer from the Daily Sentinel, Rome, when downtown Oneida was burning in the middle of the night and took the Rome job early in 1979. I'm still there. I think I'm only one of two classmates still working full-time in newspaper, the reason the program was created.

I developed an interest in hiking. Running didn't sound like much fun so I pull on a pack with 30-40-50 pounds and walk, then jump in a lake at the end -- much more fun.

As chair of the Iroquois Chapter of the Adirondack Mountain Club, I got to know publications staff at headquarters. They approached me about updating one of the club's trail guidebooks so I pushed a measuring wheel, took notes and tracked myself with a GPS for years, offering some third edition updates and eventually a rewrite to create the fourth edition of "Adirondack Trails: West-Central Region" (see www.adk.org).

The map that goes along with the book, and distances of trail segments described in the book, were used by another outfit to create bigger maps. I was among the guidebook authors asked to review the draft of those maps. My name isn't on them, and I didn't get sent around the world, but that's how my childhood idea came to fruition – I was doing a job for National Geographic.

Norm Landis, of the first journalism class at Morrisville (1969), received bachelor's degrees from SUNY Utica-Rome in 1984 (business) and 1988 (computer information science) but continues work in the field of his associate's degree. He's a state-licensed outdoor guide, state-certified search crew boss, co-treasurer of his church, and "distinguished alumnus" of SUNY Utica-Rome. He's a member of the Iroquois Chapter, Adirondack Mountain Club; the Tramp and Trail Club of Utica, and the New York State Outdoor Guides Association.

Norm Landis '69   **Norm Landis today**

9

The Day of the Kent State Massacre

By Joanne Brogan
Class of 1972

The Vietnam War was being protested at Morrisville Ag and Tech by a small but dedicated group of students. Some of us had participated in a candlelight march at Syracuse University in the fall of 1969 and protested at the Rome Air Force Base. A few of the leaders of the Morrisville Political Action Committee were, in fact, veterans returned from Vietnam.

We had sat in East Hall's small lounge in December 1969 for the birthday draft lottery. Every girl in that dorm was there to see how her boyfriend or brother's birthday would fall in the lottery. Those whose birthdays were drawn early were certain to be drafted. We all hoped our loved ones would be called at the end.

The only time I remember as many girls in that tiny room was for Tiny Tim's wedding to Miss Vicky. What a contrast in content for television viewing!

On April 30, 1970 President Nixon announced the invasion of Cambodia. His actions caused a huge protest on most college campuses across the nation.

A few days later – May 4 – had been a beautiful spring day on campus. I was in Seneca Dining Hall when one of my fellow Journalism students broke the news of the shooting of students at Kent State University in Ohio. It was one of those moments that are forever fixed in my mind, like the assassination of John Kennedy or the events of my 50th birthday – September 11, 2001. My reaction to the news was visceral. I felt that it could have been me that was dead on a grassy knoll on a college campus.

After collecting my thoughts I realized that I was scheduled to host a show on WCVM that afternoon. My task then was to borrow the albums I would need. I now planned to do an hour of nothing but anti-war music. There was plenty to choose from. The songs that come to mind now are Joni Mitchell's "The Fiddle and The Drum," Joan Baez' "Minister of War," Bob Dylan "Blowin' In the Wind," "War" by Edwin Starr, and, of course, "The Fish Cheer/Feel Like I'm Fixin' To Die" by Country Joe MacDonald and the Fish. At that time WCVM was in the basement of Oneida Hall and not recognized by the FCC.

There was a meeting at Hamilton Hall that day to discuss the action that would be taken at MATC. Many students decided to join the nationwide student strike. There are photos in "The Arcadian" of these students. The bell was removed from Madison Hall to toll each time the name of a soldier who had already died was read. The recitation went on for 24 hours a day for several days and there was a tent set up on the lawn of Bailey Annex to house the readers.

Life for college students in this country changed that day. I don't think we felt the same way about our lives, our safety and our government after that day.

I remember the events in Ohio every year on May 4. We should not forget.

Joanne Brogan attended Morrisville Ag & Tech from 1969 -1972. She furthered her education at Mercy College, Dobbs Ferry, NY and obtained a B.S. in Accounting in 1981. Her first job after MATC was for WOR-AM radio, where she worked in the sales and traffic departments. Most recently she has been employed by the City School District of New Rochelle as a Financial Analyst.

She is married to Jerre Holbrook and lives in City Island, NY. She has three grandchildren and enjoys traveling, cooking, some crafts, and is addicted to genealogy.

(AP Photo)

SECTION 2

The Stories We Have Covered

10

Jack Durschlag '81 Wins Pulitzer

By Michael Gormley
Class of 1981

In the basement of the STUAC building this fall night in 1980, The Chimes staff was in the throes of meeting deadline. At a desk in the middle of it all, among the greasy potato chip bags and empty diet soda cans, was Jack Durschlag, carefully editing. As he did every week, he would make the article he worked on clearer and more relevant to readers.

Twenty-five years later, those high standards and Durschlag's laser focus would help his newspaper, the Star-Ledger of Newark, win a Pulitzer Prize. The staff won journalism's most coveted award for extensive and immediate coverage of the resignation of New Jersey's governor after he announced he was "a gay American," and he had committed adultery with a man. It was the newspaper's second Pulitzer in 173 years.

One of Durschlag's first calls after the celebration was to Jerry Leone. "I called Jerry after this happened... I told him none of this could have been done without his efforts," said Durschlag. "Every day I thank God I was at Morrisville at the right time and learned what was needed to be done and what was needed to put out a newspaper."

Back in the STUAC basement 25 years ago, there was no time to dream of Pulitzers as deadline loomed. To Durschlag, deadlines were serious. "I remember from his work on The Chimes that he was a diehard staff member," said Denise Snyder, the Chimes editor from 1980-81. "He hung in there no matter what—a trait that I'm sure has helped contribute to his success," said Snyder.

Hanging in there was exactly what the staff of the 450,000-circulation daily had to do that late August day when the governor called a surprise press conference. With half the metro staff on vacation—including two top political journalists—the staff grabbed sources and chased down tips.

By the time the long day was over, the Star-Ledger had 10 pages of stories and sidebars. Jack, who began the work day at 2:30 p.m., didn't get home until nearly 2 a.m. the next day.

The work Durschlag put into his career is clear. After graduating from Morrisville in 1981, he earned his bachelor's degree from the State University at Albany. His career began as a copy editor for the American Institute of Physics, followed by a reporting job at the Oneida Daily Dispatch until 1986. He was an editorial writer and layout editor for the North Jersey Advance and worked at the Morristown Daily Record in Parsippany, N.J. from 1987-92. From there, he joined the Star-Ledger. Along the way, the native of Hicksville, N.Y., raised a family with his wife, Amy. They have two children—Rachel and Laryssa.

His journalist's journey hasn't been easy, but the good times strongly outweigh the bad. "You have to want it. That's the thing. It has to be full throttle forward to try to make your career important to you, and then you can change people's lives. You really do," he said.

Former New Jersey Governor Jim McGreevey announces in 2004, "I am a gay American."

11

Racing to Saratoga

By Tony Podlaski
Class of 1994

While I was covering the first round of the NCAA Division I men's lacrosse tournament for the Baltimore Sun in May, I asked myself two questions: why was I at this game and how did I get here? The answer came quickly: Morrisville.

It's amazing how much of an impact Morrisville's journalism program, guided by the best quartet I have ever met – Jerry Leone, Neal Bandlow, Mary Ellen Mengucci and Brian McDowell, can have on someone's life. When I came to Morrisville in August 1992, this foursome helped me change my life.

Along with teaching the skills needed for journalism—whether it was writing a feature story, editing, taking pictures or learning about the Federal Communication Commission—Jerry, Neal, Mary Ellen and Brian taught me about life—both on and off campus. They also guided and advised me to be not only a successful student, but also a successful individual.

Perhaps the most valuable advice I received from them was my career path. While I was taking journalism courses and being the executive editor of *The Chimes*, I had aspirations of being a sportswriter (Neal even helped me get a part-time job for the sports department of the *Oneida Daily Dispatch*). Because of my academic success after the first year at Morrisville, Jerry, Neal, Mary Ellen and Brian suggested I should tutor the freshman class for the midterm exam. After they had seen me tutor some of the students, who later passed that exam, they said I should consider teaching because I was able to reach the students effectively. Initially, I couldn't take their advice seriously because it wasn't in my career path. Later, I learned their advice was more valuable than that which they had presented in each class lesson.

After I graduated early from Morrisville, I was hired as a part-time staff writer and assistant for the sports department of the *Albany Times Union*. Simultaneously, I was selected as one of the top 50 students in the country to participate in the Kentucky Derby Sports Journalism seminar.

Over the three-day seminar, I had learned about writing well-developed sports stories, conducting effective interviews and making contacts in a very competitive field. But one of the more important things I really learned through that experience was the amount of respect the Morrisville journalism program had received from the members of the sports media and students in four-year journalism programs like Missouri, Arizona State, Colorado, West Virginia, Maryland, and others. It was this amount of respect that has given me other job opportunities in the media field.

Since I graduated from Morrisville 13 years ago, I have written for various newspapers throughout the country, including the Orlando Sentinel, the Denver Post and the Pittsburgh Tribune. At the same time, I have worked as a media relations assistant for the New York Racing Association, where I have been privileged to witness the best racing in the country, including the Belmont and Breeders' Cup Thoroughbred Championships. I've even had the opportunity to interview one of my childhood idols, Hall of Fame catcher Gary Carter.

Today, along with freelancing and working at the Times Union, I teach writing and literature to junior-college students at Hudson Valley Community College. My teaching philosophy reflects the teaching philosophy of Jerry, Neal, Mary Ellen, and Brian. The knowledge and passion these four individuals brought into the classroom is the same approach I take in my teaching. I thank you and the other mentors (past, present and future), as well as alumni, for keeping the Journalism program going for 40 years.

Tony Podlaski, of the New York Racing Association, puts Bluegrass Cat on the board during the Travers Draw on Wednesday, Aug. 23, 2006 at Saratoga Springs, N.Y.

12

Six Years Erased False Notions

By Cary B. Ziter
Class of 1974

In my six strange and savage years as a radio and daily newspaper reporter, I don't recall meeting anyone famous or covering a single story with lasting impact. I do remember, however, spending a great deal of time on the edge, fighting with management for a larger pay check—that, and wondering why the City Desk wouldn't let me cover a rock concert, knowing I would subsequently submit an expense account for a long list of hideous chemicals.

Most of the people I interacted with as a reporter worked for local governments in Albany and Schenectady Counties, upstate New York. A large portion of these devoted servants spent their time chewing gum and looking out the window. Despite the predatory power of the First Amendment, they answered few of my questions. When they did answer, the replies were ugly, senseless; a teary saga from a vagrant land.

So much of my time at the typewriter amounted to a louse-ladled frenzy, a boiling trip to the upper colon of American society. It was a place dark and desperate where I was called on to outline Truth, but had no idea what it looked like or why people would swallow my version of it. Confused, I finally tossed the trade for health benefits and a car that would start every morning.

One thing reporting did give me, however, is this: it stripped away all false notions about humanity. After years of inexplicably long and sad government meetings, police reports filled with cruel, heartless acts, and dreaded interviews with monstrous, evil shopkeepers, I knew the world to be what it was: a shaved and perfumed wart hiding behind a cloud of dandruff, halitosis and social strain.

Looking back on my journalism career four decades later, I have to say that's not a bad lesson. A young, mentally inferior lad should somehow be introduced to the fact that the world isn't always marvelous, that it's far more volcano than vitality, a nest of hot licking flames accented with the disgusting gurgling of conniving animals lingering in nearby shadows.

Despite this, I struggle to imagine what I would have done smartly in my early days if I had not become a reporter. The routine of a fry cook or a used car salesman might have taken me to great heights, I suppose. And to this day, I follow the news industry closely.

That's because I lecture in communications at a four-year college, where I tell my students that modern journalism, it seems to me, falls somewhere between the work of cannibals and people who relish scrubbing their privates in public. Recommending such work as a living to someone who isn't off their rocker is getting harder to justify.

Then again, as Raoul Duke noted at the height of Gonzo, "I wouldn't recommend sex, drugs or insanity for everyone, but they've always worked for me." And, with a kind of jack of hearts smile, I can truly borrow from that thought to say the same about the role of journalism in my lucky little life.

CARY B. ZITER followed his act at Morrisville with a BA in political science from SUNY Albany and a Master's in literature from Bennington College. He worked in corporate public relations for more than a quarter century, retiring from IBM in 2006. He's currently a teaching assistant for a vocational-technical high school and serves as an adjunct professor at Mount Saint Mary College, Newburgh, N.Y.

13

Miracle On Ice to Oneida Indian Nation

By R. Patrick Corbett
Class of 1969

A photo of the St. Joan of Arc Church fire in Morrisville earned me my first check from a newspaper, the Syracuse Herald Journal.

I was coming back from the Carolina (the "I"), the night of Feb. 10, 1969, munching on some meatballs left over from the sub shop where I worked, when I stumbled onto it around 7:45. Thanks to Jerry's expert conditioning, I grabbed a camera, shot the fire and called Syracuse. They were delighted and paid, as I recall, $10.

That was invested at the "I" a short time later.

In the following 40 or so years, I had some wonderful professional and personal opportunities, like the 1980 Olympics Miracle on Ice game (also in February) and the interview with the American commander in Mogadishu (in January, but decidedly warmer in Somalia) warning of disaster unless the warlords were disarmed—four months before the Blackhawk Down incident.

There are indelible scenes like NYC the day after the 9/11 attacks, pine boughs imbedded in the flaps of a B-52 after a low-level practice bombing mission in Maine, and watching over a sketch artist's shoulder (no cameras allowed) as eight Supreme Court justices pondered the Oneida Indian Nation's taxable status.

High in that pantheon of memories are the hundreds of faces of men, women and children, laughing in joy or twisted in physical or emotional pain at so many scenes of everyday wonders and disasters.

And I owe it to Jerry.

I signed up for journalism because my first choice course was full for the fall semester and I had some success with creative writing in high school. Jerry Leone had me mesmerized by the end of the semester and talked me out of transferring over to wood tech.

The rat. I could own my own lumber yard by now—or be working for Home Depot .

Instead, I've got (literally) a world of great experiences under my belt, and I can afford to have somebody else build my log cabin.

Thanks a lot, Jer.

R. Patrick Corbett retired after 37 years with the Utica Observer-Dispatch. He is now helping Mohawk Valley Community Action with media relations, newsletters, Web site, and training, and he's a volunteer coordinator for a 1930's restored gas station museum in Rome (Come visit anytime). He is still married after all these years (38) and living in Rome.

Corbett with his daughter, Colleen (to soften the image)

14

Pulitzer Nomination:
Possible Mob Ties to Dairy

By James B. Flateau
Class of 1970

It was only natural that I would wind up in the journalism program at Morrisville.

In my senior year at Tonawanda High School near Buffalo, I was one of 15 students taking this real cool journalism course. After the semester ended in May 1967, I planned to work for a year to gather some of the shekels needed to afford a college offering journalism.

My high school journalism teacher said, "Not to worry." It was going to take him a year, anyway, to get settled into his new job—creating the journalism program at Morrisville.

So I spent the next year following where Jerry Leone had already been: I worked at the Tonawanda Evening News. Jerry had worked there as a swing editor during the summers while teaching high school.

I then followed him to Morrisville in the Fall of 1968. It was as comfortable a transition from Jerry the Teacher to Jerry the Professor as ... well, as slipping into a well-worn pair of white bucks.

A teacher by profession and local newspaper editor by vocation, Jerry knew the skills and abilities that we had to nurture to make it as hacks and flacks. He designed a program which Syracuse University J-students were only experiencing in their junior and senior years.

I was recruited while at Morrisville by Ottaway Newspapers, Inc. I worked my way up from reporter to news editor at their Oneonta daily newspaper. I was appointed Albany Bureau Chief, writing from the state capitol on all facets of government for five Ottaway newspapers. It was during this period that my series on possible mob ties to a dairy cooperative was submitted by Ottaway for the Pulitzer Prize.

After 14 years with Ottaway, Gov. Mario Cuomo asked me to serve as spokesman for the Department of Correctional Services. (This was in addition to my role as counselor and advisor to the governor and prison commissioner). After then-state Sen. George Pataki defeated Cuomo, the new governor asked me to remain as his prison spokesman. I stayed for a total of 21 years, becoming the first spokesman promoted to the rank of assistant commissioner.

I had two years at Morrisville and then two employers in a career spanning 35 years. That sounded about right: one career for each year at Morrisville.

My schooling and careers owe a great debt to my friend, teacher and mentor, Jerry Leone. It is a testament to his love for teaching and students that the lives he touched and guided have taken so many positive and disparate paths across this nation.

Thanks, Chief.

Jim and his "beloved Rita" decided to relocate from upstate New York to the south—but not, "as some wags say, because Jerry had done so years earlier with his beautiful bride Barbara."

Jim reports that Florida is home to Rita's "wonderful daughter and son-in-law, and their precious and delightful daughters Lila and Julia."

He sends his regards to all.

15

9/11

By Jim Johnson
Class of 1978

Sometimes the biggest and most important stories begin in your own backyard. Sunday, September 9, 2001 dawned brilliantly on Long Island. My wife breathed a sigh of relief to see the clear skies because she had invited a group of family and friends over for a barbecue to celebrate my birthday that would occur just two days hence.

By early afternoon the kids were jumping in the pool, the cheese was dripping down the burgers on the grill, and my dad was reaching into the cooler for another cold Bud. Suddenly he snapped to and said, "Before I forget, what are you doing on Tuesday? I need a fourth for golf."

I would have loved to join the old guy for a round on the links, but I had previously scheduled early morning-meetings for that Tuesday at Montefiore Hospital in the Bronx. I explained to my dad that those meetings led into a presentation I was making on September 12 at a technology conference at Windows on the World at the top of the World Trade Center.

Rebuffed but undaunted, he turned to my younger brother, Pete, a Port Authority cop based at JFK Airport in Queens. "What about you? Do you want to jump in?" my dad asked. My brother thought for a moment and said, "You know, I haven't taken a day off in a while… Sure, I'd love to join you."

So early on the morning of September 11th, I was delivering a presentation in a doctor's office in the Bronx and my dad and brother were on a golf course on Long Island. They would later recall looking up from their putts and noticing a large plume of smoke in the sky to the west. My brother remembered thinking, "must be one of those fuel tanks at the refineries in Staten Island or New Jersey going up…"

As the second plane piloted by terrorists aimed for the World Trade Center the Port Authority Police Department was already in the midst of calling every available man in to their assigned posts. The PA is exclusively

34

responsible for patrolling all of the bridges and tunnels around New York City, plus the area airports and the World Trade Center. My brother's partner, George Howard, had been at home when he got the call to report immediately to JFK Airport. He called my brother's house with the intent of picking him up and car-pooling to the airport. My sister-in-law explained that she had already called the golf course and that the pro was on his way out to find my brother. George said, "I'm going to go on ahead. Tell Pete to meet me as soon as he can…"

By the time my brother got off the golf course and made his way to JFK, his partner had already left on a truck toward the place we'd soon call Ground Zero. My brother hopped on the next truck and joined the trail of heroes heading toward the unknown.

Within a few minutes, a call came that one of the towers had collapsed and it had taken out the Port Authority fire truck where George Howard and several other heroes had been working. My brother's heart sank. After taking a few minutes to compose himself, he knew there was only one thing to do. His truck arrived on the scene and his team spent the next several hours digging by hand in an attempt to recover their fallen comrades. When they found George's stilled body, my brother removed his partner's shield and drove to Howard's mother's house on Long Island. He presented the shield to her along with his deepest condolences.

For the next week, my brother joined groups of volunteers who spent time digging through the rubble, hoping for survivors, but expecting the worst. On September 20th he sat down on his couch, and joined most Americans, as we watched George Bush address a joint session of Congress.

As the president neared the end of his 40-minute speech, he said, "It is my hope that in the months and years ahead, life will return almost to normal. We'll go back to our lives and routines, and that is good. Even grief recedes with time and grace. But our resolve must not pass. Each of us will remember what happened that day, and to whom it happened. We'll remember the moment the news came—where we were and what we were doing. Some will remember an image of a fire, or a story of rescue. Some will carry memories of a face and a voice gone forever."

He continued, "And I will carry this: It is the police shield of a man named George Howard, who died at the World Trade Center trying to save others. It was given to me by his mom, Arlene, as a proud memorial to her son. This is my reminder of lives that ended, and a task that does not end."

To this day, George Bush carries the shield of my brother's partner. It serves as a focal point to the president about the task at hand, but it also serves as a reminder to my brother and his family that sometimes the biggest and most important stories begin in your own backyard.

16

2004 Olympics in Athens

By Frank Isola

Class of 1984

The New York Daily News has been good to me over the years, assigning me to cover the World Series, World Cup, NBA Finals and U.S. Open tennis. I've never been to a Super Bowl, so I have no way of knowing if the NFL's media hospitality room is as impressive as everyone says.

It must be pretty good, because you only read stories about steroids in baseball—not in the league where 350-pound linemen grow on trees.

I was there when Michael Jordan hit the series-clinching shot against the Utah Jazz in 1998, and I'm still pretty sure he pushed off on Bryon Russell. I saw Derek Jeter beat the Mets by himself in the Subway World Series, and I covered the late Darryl Kile's no-hitter against the Mets in 1993.

But the most significant story I covered would have to be the 2004 Olympics. Being in Athens was an incredible experience, one that I will never forget. It made all the nonsense about this business well worth it.

There was never a day that passed when I didn't appreciate the opportunity, and I appreciated it even more when I turned off my laptop at night. (If you know what I mean).

I always enjoyed my time at Morrisville, which seems like another lifetime ago. It certainly passed too quickly.

The selfless work the professors made was quite extraordinary. They warned us that if we transferred to a four-year college, we would have a greater understanding of journalism than some of the young hot shots at these colleges. I thought they were mad, but when I attended the University of Maryland, most of the third-year journalism students could barely write their names—much less write a hard-news story about Joe Doaks being arrested for shoplifting.

The on-the-job training at Morrisville was invaluable. Trying to put out a newspaper back then was a grind, but it taught you to care for something and be responsible. That place gave me confidence that I could do anything in this profession. In recent years I've done a lot of television work, I've hosted a radio show on Sirius and I even try to fit my newspaper gig into that schedule.

I'm not sure where I'll end up, but I'll always remember where I started.

After attending the University of Maryland at College Park, Isola joined the staff of the New York Post in 1987. He covered high school and college sports before being assigned to the Mets beat in 1993. In 1994, he joined the New York Daily News, and two years later was assigned to the Knicks' beat, a job he currently holds.

Isola co-authored a book with Mike Wise (a columnist with the Washington Post). The book "Just Ballin...The Chaotic Rise of the New York Knicks," was published in 2000. He's written for several Web sites and magazines and is a regular contributor for NBA TV and SNY in New York. He is also the co-host of "Tip-Off," a morning show on NBA Radio on Sirius.

He is the recipient of an Associated Press Sports Editors (APSE) sports writing award and has been recognized by the New York chapter of the Deadline Club.

Frank lives in Montclair, N.J. with his wife and two children.

Professor John O'Connor

17

Breaking News—Sauter's Diner Fire

By Mike Gormley
Class of 1981

On an April night in 1980, Sauter's Diner and bowling alley in Morrisville was on fire.

Several journalism students rushed to the scene, covered the Route 20 landmark as it burned to a black shell, then rushed back to campus. By the time that long Tuesday night was over, there was a rarity in The Chimes: A breaking story from hours before with a strong photo. The same Chimes reporters also had the story for the Wednesday morning papers in Oneida and Syracuse, thanks to a hell-bent drive on dark country roads.

The next morning at the 8 a.m. Editing class of John O'Connor in the Lab Classroom Building, I told the hard-nosed, former Washington Post staffer about the reporting and the drive to get the story right and in the morning newspapers.

``That's what you're supposed to do," he said, and walked away.

Through more than 25 years in daily journalism since, I remembered that and other Morrisville journalism lessons not contained in text books.

When I went undercover within a band of survivalists with automatic weapons that scared the hell out of the locals because that was the only way to get the story, I thought of the drive Jerry Leone taught us.

When I was in Saudi Arabia for Hearst News Service covering Operation Desert Shield and made an important contact with a major who was a Vietnam veteran, I thought of the perspective Neal Bandlow gave us.

When I was covering a Philadelphia-based organized crime family in Binghamton and found records that linked members to unions on a federal highway job before the FBI did, I thought of the preparation Joe Quinn had demanded of us.

38

And when I finished a six-day, 18-hours-a-day trip from Buffalo to Long Island to Manhattan as The Associated Press' reporter covering the governor's race last year, I thought of John O'Connor.

...Man, that's a lot of first-person stuff. It would never have gotten a good grade in Newswriting II. But I know my career hasn't been about me. I am surrounded by better writers, smarter people, and by competitors with the kind of buy-ya-a-beer personality that is far better suited to a life of reporting.

But Morrisville gave us all an edge.

The little Ag and Tech college gave us a critical advantage over most of the Ivy Leaguers and those holders of master's-of-whatever degrees out there. It came to me yesterday, a fairly typical day in the life of daily journalism in which no day is typical.

I started the day in the Capitol office of The Associated Press after stopping for a quick chat with a top staffer for Gov. Eliot Spitzer. I then rushed off to a news conference with Spitzer. From there I ran to the news conference of the Senate majority leader, already in progress.

From there I briefly returned to the capitol office to join a teleconference with the state education commissioner. Then I called some of my contacts who really know what's going on. I quickly read and analyzed a couple dozen very dense decisions by a state appeals court to see if there was any news there. There wasn't.

I took a few moments during phone calls to continue to analyze 500 pages of documents I obtained for a national project with a Friday deadline.

That's when a source called and tipped me that Spitzer had quietly made a deal with an Indian tribe to build a new casino. By 7 p.m., 10 hours straight after I started the day, I was done.

And happy.

That's because for a Morrisville-trained reporter, journalism isn't about being famous or rich or having a boat on the lake and margaritas at night. Journalism is more of a religion for us. I still see days like this as a day I made a difference.

Thanks, Jerry and Neal and crew, for this wonderful, frustrating, ass-busting life.

But that's what we're supposed to do.

Mike Gormley is the Capitol Editor for the Associated Press.

18

Fraudulent Trash Haulers

By Jim Kenyon
Class of 1969

The phone rang on a spring day in 1991. Little did I know that the focus of my journalism career was about to change.

By then, I had been a television news reporter for 21 years. The voice on the other end said he must remain anonymous and asked if I was still interested in investigating the garbage industry in the Syracuse area. In the late '80's, I had won several awards for covering an FBI probe into price fixing among several trash hauling companies. My source revealed that even while these companies were under a federal microscope, they were still involved in another fraudulent enterprise, truck weighting.

In Onondaga County, garbage trucks and roll-off containers were registered by their "tare" or empty weights. So when they cross the scales at the dumping stations, the tare weight would be subtracted from the full weight and the hauler would be charged for the appropriate amount of trash. But my source revealed that one company in particular secretly placed heavy metal weights beneath the trucks to give a false tare weight. Once they took the weight off, the hauler could slip tons of garbage and refuse across the scales without paying.

I set about investigating the claim. It's become second nature to me as a journalist, but I relied on the lessons learned from my days at Morrisville and Professor Jerry Leone's insistence about good old-fashioned legwork. In television that actually works quite well. Sometimes it's important to show how a story develops.

In this case, I had to research years of printouts and receipts that were stored above one of the county's dumping stations in a room called the "dust bowl". The records were literally covered by years of dust, but they revealed how the tare weights of many trash trucks and containers would greatly vary from one year to the next.

I was able to locate and interview a former heavy equipment operator who actually placed the weights on the trucks. I confronted the company's owner with camera rolling who threw me off his property, and ran the story.

The next day, the FBI and the New York State Police launched a major investigation. Within a few months, executives of five trash hauling companies had pleaded guilty to numerous charges, sentenced to Federal prisons and ordered to pay $1 million in restitution. About 35 County employees lost their jobs after pleading guilty to accepting bribes. The Resource Recovery Agency changed its disposal system to combat fraud.

The stories won several local, state and national awards, including one from the IRE (Investigative Reporters and Editors), one of the most coveted awards for investigative journalism in the world. The IRE is an arm of the University of Missouri. The trash hauling story kicked my career as a journalist into high gear. I now head the "I-Team" at WSTM-TV. There have been many other stories and numerous awards, but more importantly, I feel my work has helped my audience to make Central New York a better place.

I remember after the award presentation back in 1992, the various winners were honored at a reception during the IRE convention. Some of the top investigative reporters in the world were there talking about this and that, including where they earned their degrees. When the conversation turned to me, I proudly said, "SUNY Morrisville." They seemed puzzled. One woman said, "Oh, I never heard of it."

I thought to myself, "Now you have."

Jim is the chief investigative reporter for the Action News I-Team at WSTM in Syracuse. He has won numerous awards for his investigative reports from the Syracuse Press Club, NYS Broadcasters Association and even the U.S. Justice Department. He has served as commencement speaker at his alma mater. He has been married for 28 years and has a daughter living in NYC.

**Jim Kenyon at WSTM-TV
in Syracuse.**

19

They Tried to Burn Down My House

By Corey Hutchins
Class of 2002

In 2005, three years after graduating from Morrisville State College, I co-founded the *Columbia City Paper*, a 20,000-circulation edgy, alternative newsweekly in Columbia, South Carolina. It took less than a year before someone tried to burn down my house. The police blamed the arson on my involvement with the paper, and it became national news. That week, Ted Rall referred to my two-bedroom apartment in his syndicated column as "Ground Zero" in the assault on journalism.

I remembered then what a former J-school professor had told me at Morrisville when I first mentioned my plans to move South. "I don't think they'll take your sense of humor well down there," she said. "I think you'll be killed."

That makes for great copy.

But journalism isn't supposed to be dangerous; it's supposed to be fun, and it wasn't until later that I realized how being a good reporter can, and should, be both.

Since then I've edited the scrappy, iconoclastic newspaper with ruthless passion in pursuit of the idea that dissent protects democracy and believing without compromise in the spirit of a free and independent expression of ideas.

And I like my job.

As a journalist, I've participated in crack deals and watched football games from the governor's private skybox. I've tracked underground graffiti artists through sewer drains and seedy public officials through City Hall. I've shaken hands with those who would be president. There were bloody fatal car wrecks and as many acts of beauty. There was a loaded gun in the newsroom desk. There were sketchy cops and coked-out elected officials. There was that one invitation to a Klan meeting. There was love. There was war—on drugs and it was on terror... it was on truth.

It was between countries and it was between a little old lady and her dog catcher. There were parties and there were politics. There were disaster areas. There were love scenes and there were crime scenes. There were press passes, deadlines, and firsthand accounts. There were negative bank statements. And there was always free booze. There was blood, sweat, tears and printing ink; there was justice and there was "just us."

I tell people that I went to one of the best two-year journalism schools in the country and I think of my time at Morrisville with charming nostalgia. It was small and insulated, but it was a magical place to be at that moment in time—as planes slammed again and again into buildings on every classroom TV.

Journalism is a profession needed now as much as ever. It's under attack politically and economically. Newspapers, they say, are in their death throes as the Internet creates a new media paradigm. And the forest echoes with laughter.

In an old college notebook of mine is a quote by one MSC professor.

"College," it reads. "Is the best four years of your life that you will never have any relation to later on."

For me, he wasn't talking about Morrisville.

Corey Hutchins has published numerous works of fiction and nonfiction in newspapers and magazines, and was the winner of the prestigious Havilah Babcock writing award at the University of South Carolina. In 2007 he contributed to the anthology "Class Dismissed: 75 outrageous mind-expanding college exploits (and lessons that won't be on the final)" published by Random House imprint Villard Books.

He was a 2007 finalist in Rolling Stone magazine's contest "I'm from Rolling Stone." In 2005 he co-founded the "Columbia City Paper," an alternative weekly in Columbia, South Carolina. He has spoken on panels for the Society of Professional Journalists and has appeared on C-SPAN with Helen Thomas at the Center For American Progress.

He holds a journalism degree from Morrisville State College and a degree in English language and literature with a journalism cognate from USC. He is currently working on a book tracing the 2008 presidential campaign of the American Nazi Party's nominee for U.S. president.

20

"The Big Ice Storm" of '98

By Anne Richter Ashley
Class of 1975

I was just settling into the new year of 1998 in Watertown....when all of a sudden I was smack dab in the middle of a disaster—and it would be weeks before I felt grounded again.

On Wednesday afternoon, Jan. 7, 1998, our newsroom phones started ringing off the hook. North Country schools were closing early. Their weather reports indicated an ice storm was on its way. I quickly dispatched a WWNY-TV news crew to Theresa Elementary School to get video of students being dismissed early. The crew returned with video of children boarding buses. We had interviews with school officials who said "They weren't taking any chances." Our "live" signal on the 6 p.m. news was iffy at best but we went with it anyway because it showed a storm in the making. By the end of that newscast.....ice was beginning to form. The live truck and crew made a slow trip back to the television station.

I left for the evening feeling uneasy. When I got home, I phoned the head of the Office of Emergency Management. He was feeling uncomfortable too. His reports indicated significant icing was expected. We discussed how far reaching the storm would be. I immediately called the newsroom and directed the night crew to his house for an interview and suggested they put together a report for the 11 p.m. News on what to do in the event of a power outage. While I watched that report I DID NOT shut off our computer, microwave or stereo and I didn't, as had been suggested, gather together candles and flashlights. But I did pack an overnight bag, and I went to bed early.

Good thing! The phone rang at 4:30 a.m. It was our assignment editor. He confirmed my worst fears. Yes, the storm had materialized and the situation was getting worse by the moment. I asked him if I had time to take a shower. He paused. I knew what that meant. But I also knew that I'd be going "on the air". So, I took the shortest shower on record. I didn't even wash my hair.

The trip into the station was something I'll always remember. Watertown looked like an atomic bomb had been dropped on it. I now know what 'nuclear winter' looks like. It's devastating.

The newsroom was a madhouse. It would remain that way for days.

We had power. We used our computers to write stories, our edit decks to edit videotape and we provided our viewers with spectacular pictures and eyewitness reports. We were in crisis mode. And, then the power went out! The entire station was in the dark. Our computers were silent, we no longer had access to the outside world via Associated Press, CBS and CNN. We were a world unto ourselves. Our engineers rigged up several generators—one of them through our live truck—so live reports were now out of the question. That was okay because we couldn't navigate our huge rig through city streets that were plugged with power lines and trees.

We improvised. The 6 p.m. news script was written longhand by candlelight. A makeshift studio was set up in the control room, one of three rooms powered by our generators. We did an extended 6 p.m. newscast. I anchored wearing a gray suit, knee socks and hiking boots. There was no time to primp. We were smack-dab in the middle of a disaster, and you could tell by my hairdo!

The hours became days and even weeks. There was no time to worry about the growing puddles of water in my basement, the tremendous damage to my backyard, the thawing meat in my freezer. It would be a while before I could tend to my own ice storm problems.

First the ice, then the rain. Two days of torrential downpours. Rivers were rising as quickly as the ice was melting. The "Ice Storm Recovery" quickly turned into "Flood Watch." The Black and Oswegatchie Rivers were rising. We watched families leave their homes by boat, farmers leading their herds to higher ground, and we watched the water consume everything in its path. In Watertown, the river was raging out of control. The roar of the water was so loud you had to shout to be heard. The flooding was about to set records. And we were there to capture history in the making.

Shelters began filling with people. The president declared a federal disaster. The governor came north. He was followed by the head of the Federal Emergency Management Agency. A steady stream of politicians traveled here to see how an ice storm could devastate an entire region. The state mobilized a force of thousands to help. And we were grateful.

I'll always be proud of how the 7News team pulled together in a crisis, working long hours under very difficult conditions, without complaining. We weathered the storm together. But one ice storm in a lifetime is enough. Please!

Anne has been at WWNY-TV in Watertown, NY since 1980 and wears many hats at the station. She is Assistant News Director and also produces and co-anchors the premier newscast, "7News at 6". She still has many friends from her Morrisville days. Despite being scattered throughout the U.S., they still try to get together regularly. She said, "Morrisville was a great experience for me ... one that I treasure."

21

The Birdsall Murder Case

By Elizabeth E. (Williams) Moran
Class of 1998

Welcome to the real world. In my case, it was my first reporting job, working for a little daily evening paper in Hornell, New York, where I was the youngest, most inexperienced reporter on the staff.

As the new reporter, I never expected to get the big assignments. So imagine my surprise that first month sitting in the newsroom when my editor, Andy Thompson, looked over and said, "Liz, you can take this one."

"This one" turned out to be the Birdsall murder.

The Birdsall murder involved three people, one victim, a wooded area and a possible domestic dispute. I had no idea where to begin.

"Call the Wayne County D.A.(District Attorney)," Thompson suggested.

Back at my desk, I confidently dialed the number. I could do this, I told myself. After all, Morrisville had prepared me for this type of story. All I had to do was just remember all of professor Neal Bandlow's lectures from News Writing 1. My confidence lasted right up until the D.A. picked up the phone. This wasn't a classroom exercise; this was the real thing. Nervous, I managed to muddle through. Hanging up with a sigh of relief, I was sure I had gotten everything I needed.

I returned to the editor Thompson, giving him the details. "What kind of guns did they use?" Thompson asked.

I was speechless. It never crossed my mind to ask about the type of guns.

"Call him back," he said, calmly.

So I did, beginning with "I'm sorry to bother you again, but I have one more question..."

Afterward, as I started to begin writing my story, Thompson chimed in again, "Who were the guns registered to?"

I couldn't believe it -- another question I had failed to ask.

This went on a few more times. But finally, by deadline, I had my story written and the D.A.'s phone number memorized.

That afternoon we had heard that the Alfred-Almond judge was going to close the arraignment for the three murder suspects. Thompson told me to go down to the courthouse the next morning and demand that the arraignment remain open to the press. Don't worry, he told me. Should I be held in contempt, he vowed the paper would bail me out. No problem, I thought. I was ready to fight for an open arraignment.

Ultimately, it didn't get that far. The next day, Thompson ended up accompanying me, along with the paper's attorney, to the courthouse, where I remained outside, taking photos of the suspects entering.

The whole episode did prove to be a valuable life lesson, though. The real world teaches you that you still have a lot to learn, but I also knew for sure that Morrisville had provided a solid foundation on which to take those first steps.

Elizabeth is now a graphic designer at the Connecticut Post.

22

Exposing A Serial Rapist in Atlanta

By Anne Murray Mozingo
Class of 1982

Out of thousands of stories, I scan my memory for the most significant story I covered in my journalism career. Could it be the U.S. Supreme Court's decision on desegregation of schools? Or exposés on child abuse? They were powerful, but not like when I was a young police reporter for a mid-sized daily and I discovered a metropolitan Atlanta police department was withholding police reports from the daily stack given to reporters. My source, the director of the rape crisis center, said that four women from the same apartment complex had been raped in less than a month.

Immediately I met with the police chief and asked for comment for the next day's paper. Surprised, he said the sensitive cases were concealed because the police had been "close" to an arrest for the past two weeks. Then two more women were raped.

My articles informing the neighborhood that a dangerous man walked among them likely saved more women from being victimized, and alerted the community that their police department might not be so trusted to "protect and serve." Vital changes in the management of the department followed, as well as the arrest of the serial rapist. That felt good.

While reading musty old clips in a 20-year-old, overstuffed briefcase to check the above facts, my mother called. I told her I was writing an essay for Morrisville on the most significant story I've covered and she immediately replied: Bill's death. Of course, how could I forget? After my son was born in 1998, I quit my senior reporting job on the Seacoast of New Hampshire to freelance. For 15 months, I wrote "Labor of Love," a column on the highs and lows of parenting.

But when my dear husband, Bill Mozingo, died unexpectedly at the age of 42, my light column on motherhood turned into a column on grief.

My editor suggested I take a vacation from the column. Then one night while I was nursing my boy, the first column just poured out of me. I filed it. And for 19 months, I poured my heart out on the Family page. I described the shock, the numbness and the utter darkness that followed. The response was incredible.

My readers kept me alive, it seemed, by sending letters, books and emails to cheer me on. Some months I would hear from 30 people who understood the grip grief had on me. Before Bill's death, when I was writing stories of parents in love, I received only 5 notes about breastfeeding.

Writing about my pain was provocative. But like all good stories, this series had to end. My editor was uncomfortable with grief, like so many people, and told me after 19 months, to return to writing about motherhood. I was so distraught; I couldn't go back to being funny. I sent more than 100 letters from readers to the executive editor and publisher, asking to move the column to another section. They both agreed the column was well read, but never bothered to move it. Seven years after Bill's death, I still meet people who know me from that column and tell me how it impacted their lives.

Writing about my pain was so far removed from my years of focus on hard news, when I wouldn't sign a petition or even display a bumper sticker on my car so as not to reveal any personal opinions. Yet my most private secrets became fodder for my column. How ironic…

Anne Murray Mozingo graduated form SUNY Morrisville in 1982. She has worked as a reporter and editor for newspapers and magazines in Georgia and New England, and is currently writing "Love Never Dies," a spiritual memoir about all the amazing things that have happened since that fateful day in 2000. She lives with her son, Wyatt, in Cape Neddick, Maine. She can be reached at annemurraymozingo@maine.rr.com.

**Jerry Leone with NBC News anchor John Chancellor at
a journalism conference on Watergate in 1973.**

- Photo by Joe Traver, '72

SECTION 3

The People We Have Covered

23

President William Jefferson Clinton

By Frank Eltman
Class of 1978

I have been pretty damn lucky in a nearly 30-year journalism career to witness some pretty extraordinary events and meet some incredible people.

There was the time I visited the late Elaine Steinbeck's Manhattan apartment for an interview, where she boastfully pointed out, ``There's John's Nobel Prize right there on the table!"

I had the privilege of meeting Father Mychal Judge, the first recorded victim and a hero of the Sept. 11 terror attacks, six weeks earlier when he presided over the fifth anniversary memorial for the TWA-800 tragedy on a Long Island beach.

A year after Sept. 11, I was in Federal Hall in Manhattan and witnessed the historic joint session of Congress, which returned to New York after a nearly 200-year absence as a tribute to the city.

I have chosen, however, to share an anecdote in tribute to Neal Bandlow, because it encompasses two of his great loves: politics and sports.

In the days after Bill Clinton left the White House in 2001, AP reporters were assigned to sit outside the ex-president's Chappaqua house and dutifully report the comings and goings of Bill, Hillary and Chelsea. My turn came on a wintry Saturday about a week after George W. Bush's inaugural and the day before the Super Bowl was to be contested between the Baltimore Ravens and the New York Giants.

The controversies that dogged the president in the White House followed him to Chappaqua, and we were particularly interested in what he had to say about some controversial 11th-hour pardons he signed on the way out the door.

Starting early in the morning, I stood with colleagues from the New York media on pieces of cardboard strewn along an icy side road (the cardboard was to keep our feet from freezing; it didn't help) outside the

52

Clinton compound and watched as various vehicles - mostly with dark-tinted windows - came and went. We were all desperate for any snippet of a quote from the president, or one of his staff, that we could feed back to our desks.

Waiting around, it turns out, is one of the most important things a journalist has to learn, by the way.

Finally, around 4 in the afternoon, just as it was starting to get dark (this is late January, remember), the ex-president comes sauntering down the driveway with his chocolate lab Buddy in tow. A reporter from the News or Post starts to bark a question about Mark Rich and the pardons, but Mr. Clinton appears to be incapable of hearing what is shouted.

He tosses a tennis ball down the street and Buddy dutifully fetches and returns the Spalding. Realizing that the former president has no intention of discussing politics, I decide to ask a question he MIGHT answer.

"Who do you like in the Super Bowl tomorrow, Mr. President?" He can't resist. He comes right over to the police barriers, shakes all our hands, and confides in me, ``There's no way the Giants can lose tomorrow!"

The following Monday morning, the headlines said it all:

Baltimore 34, N.Y. Giants 7

Thanks, Mr. President. Welcome to New York.

Frank Eltman has been the Long Island correspondent for The Associated Press since June 2006. He joined the AP in 1988 as an editor on the wire service's fledgling online news service and moved to the New York City bureau as a general assignment reporter in 1995. In the 1980s, he worked with many Morrisville journalism alumni who started their careers at The Oneida Daily Dispatch, first as the newspaper's sports editor and later as managing editor. He began his career at The Amityville Record in 1979.

24

Billy Joel—The Piano Man

By Mark Bialczak

Class of 1977

Here are the stories of a big fish that swam into my pond and wiggled around awhile, and an even bigger fish that eluded me even after I dove into its ocean.

As the man on the music beat for The Syracuse Post-Standard since 1991, I always attempt to land that big interview when somebody really *big's* coming to play our town. Even when I expect to hear a 'no,' I'll call the publicist and request a phone session anyway. What the heck, I figure.

So after being shooed away by Billy Joel's publicist a couple of times, I was delighted to hear the news that my fellow Long Island native would be calling me to talk about an upcoming show at the Carrier Dome. "Billy'll give you 15 minutes," she said.

Sure enough, Joel called at the appointed time, and we talked. We thoroughly covered the state of his music career -- he had just released what turned out to be his last great pop album, as it turned out -- and meandered into *LawnGuyland* stories and landmarks.

He grew up in Hicksville. I lived in the next burg over, Levittown, until eighth grade. We discovered we both swam at the public pool at the village green in between. He asked: Where does your family live now? Then his call-waiting clicked. I realized we'd been on the phone for an hour. He promised he'd call back. And he did, so we could continue discussing the state of fishing and weekend warriors out there in the Hamptons.

After we hung up, his publicist called. I told her how we'd clicked, talking like regular buddies for more than an hour. "Oh, he must have been bored this morning," she said. Pop, went my ego balloon.

I got a great Sunday magazine section Q and A out of it anyway. (OK, so there's still some air in that ego balloon).

One performer that I've never been able to talk with is my favorite musician of all-time. Once I even suggested to Bruce Springsteen's publicist that he lump all of us writers from mid-sized papers into one conference call, allowing us all one question. (Not an original idea, I must admit, because I've been included in these sessions for Britney Spears and The Backstreet Boys.) I got a compliment for trying from the publicist—and yet another turndown.

So The Post-Standard sent me and photographer Al Campanie to the Jersey shore for four days. We stuck our noses into Asbury Park and Freehold, meeting loads of folks who knew Springsteen both before and after his climb to fame. I couldn't believe how run down The Stone Pony had become. I thrilled in walking the Asbury Park boardwalk and spotting Madame Marie's anyway.

All the while, we hoped somebody would tell somebody who would tell Bruce we were down there poking around. Didn't happen.

So our Sunday spread detailing our chase was headlined "The Ghost of Bruce Springsteen," coinciding quite nicely with his "Ghost of Tom Joad" tour that was coming to the Landmark Theatre.

Springsteen's publicist asked for me to fax it to her. (Remember when that's how we communicated in business?)

Somebody must have liked it. When I got to the Landmark to pick up my review tickets, I discovered I was seated front row, center aisle.

The story had another interesting twist. Later on, I discovered that my Post-Standard review of the concert was used as the liner notes to a bootleg CD of the show.

I hope Springsteen never saw that unauthorized disc.

Mark has covered the music beat for the Syracuse Post-Standard since 1991. His "Listen Up" column is a must-read for anyone wanting to know more about the central New York music scene.

His only regret is that Peppi Marchello and The Good Rats never called back after his audition.

Mark Bialczak today

25

Bill Torrey—New York Islanders

By Jim Johnson
Class of 1978

It was 1982, and I had been working on a magazine for people who collect sports memorabilia. The couple who owned the publication decided to move the whole operation to San Diego. I went west with them for a time, but was probably the only guy alive who hated San Diego.

As I made plans to come home, a friend of mine, Mike Klein—a retired Wall Street exec—called and asked what I was going to do when I returned east. I figured I'd go back to the weekly newspaper chain I had previously worked for, or maybe apply at NEWSDAY.

He invited me to his home in Garden City and we sat on his porch, drinking a couple of beers and discussing possible business ventures. Ultimately he said, "you're a writer and I have money to invest, so why don't we start a magazine for the New York Islanders?" The Isles had just won their third straight Stanley Cup, and we didn't feel the local coverage (Newsday) was doing their feat justice.

Being 22 years old and having just walked away from a pretty nice gig, the idea sounded pretty good to me. I asked him, "How do we get things off the ground?" He said that the first thing we should do was to get the blessing of Islanders GM Bill Torrey. And with that, he walked into his house. He emerged a minute later with the phone book, dialed the Islanders' office, and asked to speak to Torrey. To this day, I still have no idea how it happened, but the switchboard operator actually patched him directly in to Torrey's office!

The next thing I knew, Mike was saying, "Mr. Torrey, you don't know me but I've got a great idea for a magazine for the Islanders." The busy executive told him that he was leaving the office in 30 minutes. He said, "if you can get here before I leave, I'll meet with you..."

Mike and I jumped in his car and started the 5-minute ride to the Nassau Coliseum. I couldn't believe that we were going to actually meet with the architect of the Islanders' dynasty! I said to Mike, "What the hell are we going to tell him?"

Mike was extremely glib, and he assured me, "Don't worry, I'll do all the talking..."

We got to the Islanders' office in light-speed and were ushered back to Torrey's imposing, mahogany-walled office. There were miniature Stanley Cups displayed on a mantle and photos from each of the Cup celebrations. This was quite heady stuff for a kid who grew up in Hicksville rooting for the team Torrey had assembled... Mike and I sat down in a couple of over-stuffed leather chairs and Torrey soon walked in.

Mike kicked it off by saying, "Mr. Torrey, thanks so much for taking this meeting on such short notice. My colleague and I have a great idea for a magazine about the Islanders, and... Jim's gonna tell you all about it..."

When I removed my jaw from my chest, I came up with a couple of ideas that must have resonated with the G.M. When I was done speaking he took a long look up and down at Mike and me and said, "I like you guys... Let's do it. See my attorney on the way out and he'll draw up the papers..."

Three months later, the first issue of Islander News rolled off the presses. Mike and I published for two years and then the Islanders approached us about taking the magazine in-house. Within a year, Torrey asked me to run the Islanders' sales and marketing operation. I stayed with the team in that capacity until 1995.

Jim is now the executive director of Pat LaFontaine's Companions in Courage Foundation (www.CiC16.org), a charity building interactive game rooms in children's hospitals throughout North America.

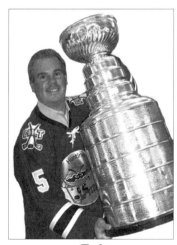

1977   **Today**

57

26

Dave Garroway—NBC's Today Show

By Bill Widell

Class of 1969

Early in my senior year at Waterloo High School, I met with a Morrisville admissions counselor. My thoughts about pursuing a program in business changed the minute he told me about the Journalism program starting in September 1967.

I had been co-editor of our junior high newspaper and my English grades were strong through high school, so it seemed a good fit for me.

Thus I was one of the students who joined Jerry Leone in Bailey Hall to kick off the Journalism program, forming lasting friendships, memories, and a solid knowledge of the working reporter's tools.

My writing grades were decent, but Photography was another story. Jerry once joked that I could one day end up as photo editor for the Wall Street Journal, which, of course, ran no photographs.

After graduation, I worked in the Public Relations Department of the National Shawmut Bank in Boston. As part of the internal communications group, I wrote press releases to be distributed within the 1,200 employee holding company that spanned Massachusetts. I was also chief writer and assistant editor of the house organ and helped organize employee events like outings to Red Sox games, the Boston Pops, and cultural sites in the Boston area.

One assignment was the judging for the Shawmut Bank "Torch Girl" who would represent the bank at the United Fund's (now the United Way) internal campaign. The celebrity judges were Dave Garroway, the founding host of NBC's Today Show; and John Taylor, publisher of the *Boston Globe*. Senior PR staff members, hoping to keep favorable relations with the top newspaper in New England, latched onto Taylor. I was given the task of interviewing Garroway prior to the judging.

Garroway arrived 30 minutes late, and the consensus that day was that he had been drinking heavily. I would later learn he battled depression

58

and some prescription drug addictions. owever, I was left to deal with the tipsy judge who at one point loudly made unflattering (and unprintable) comments about his former Chimpanzee "co-host" J. Fred Muggs. I don't recall if Taylor erred that day, but I was only allowed to mention that Garroway and Taylor were "invited" to be judges in my article about the crowning of the Torch Girl for 1970-71.

I left that job after two years to pursue my bachelor's degree, and after college, I went into bank operations management and eventually into a career in manufacturing.

In the early 90s, while doing historical research for the American Independence Museum in Exeter, NH, I found the interviewing and fact-finding skills learned in Jerry's classes were just as valuable in that pursuit as they were for news writing.

Although my days as a paid flack were limited, I feel very fortunate to have been a part of the first Journalism Class at Morrisville. Jerry Leone's influence was no doubt a factor when my son Brian, a student at Princeton University, became editor and publisher of Business Today, a national student business magazine founded by the Forbes Family.

Bill Widell earned a BS degree from Franklin Pierce College in Rindge, NH. He spent 10 years in banking, including 2 years in public relations. He has been involved in manufacturing management and consulting since 1979 in both NH and NY.

Bill is very active in non-profit organizations, having served as President of the Exeter (NH) Area Jaycees, the Southeastern NH Chapter of the International Management Council, the East Coast PRMS User Group, Acacia North American User Group and the Tri-City Chapter of APICS (American Production and Inventory Control Society) and has twice been named Tri-City member of the year. He served several years as docent and research associate for the American Independence Museum in Exeter, NH.

He currently resides in Lakewood, NY with his wife, Cathey. Their son Brian is President of Profit Tools, LLC, a developer and seller of operations software systems for the trucking industry.

27

Yoko Ono and Bernadette Devlin

By Karen (Budzynski) Knight
Class of 1975

A couple of the most prominent people I ever interviewed happened during my time at Morrisville when I met with Yoko Ono and Bernadette Devlin. Both women spoke at Colgate University in Hamilton as part of a free speakers' program, and I angled my way in for interviews. The program brought prominent and topical leaders into the community.

As Mo'ville was nearby, my friends and I thought it would be "cool" to cover these speakers and bring some of the political activism they represented into the MATC world. In the mid-70s, Yoko had been the subject of much publicity—from being called the "world's most famous unknown artist," because no one really knew what she did, to being blamed for the Beatles break up. Although surprisingly small and diminutive in real life, her image was larger than life based on her political beliefs, the "bed-in" in Amsterdam, and her connection with John Lennon.

Working with Charlie Hammond to ensure I asked the "right" questions, I was able to join a small group of journalists who interviewed her at Colgate prior to her speech. I recall that she was very melodic and understated as she talked about life with John, the War, and her work. Her cause was "world peace," yet in the middle of Vietnam, this seemed impossible. She spoke on behalf of the feminist movement, and today when you look at how far (or not) women's rights have come, she was a leader.

I also saw Bernadette Devlin as part of that series. She had been a high school hero for me, as she was a Northern Ireland Republican political activist who also was the youngest woman elected to the British Parliament. Listening to Bernadette speak was a bit more difficult because of her Irish brogue, but your ear tuned in after listening for a while.

Her 1969 book, *The Price of My Soul,* publicized the claims of Roman Catholics about discrimination in Northern Ireland. Her radical left-wing politics resulted in a conviction of incitement to riot in December 1969 because she had actively engaged, on the side of the residents, in the Battle of the Bogside, which followed that year's Apprentice Boys march and is widely marked as the beginning of Northern Ireland's 30-year "troubles."

In both of these instances, I look back on the "causes" of these women, and see how little things have changed. As activists in their own right in the '70s, these women surely would not realize how history would remember them, or that their messages would still be valid. Covering these events was important to me because of what these women stood for and represented; it's also made me reflect on how complacent we've become over time.

Karen reports that she was married, divorced and has two beautiful daughters, Andrea, 21, and Jessica, 24. Jessica married last fall and is a teacher in the Baltimore City School District. Andrea graduated from the University of Tampa this year and is a paralegal at a major Tampa law firm.

Karen now spends time with friends in Yorktown, NY and at her Cape May, NJ, beach house, enjoying the benefits of being single. She enjoys traveling, most recently visiting Cyprus, Egypt and the Great Pyramids, Kenya, the Amalfi Coast, the Isle of Capri, and many other national and international cities.

1975

With her daughters today

28

Elie Wiesel

By Liza Frenette
Class of 1978

Spending several hours with author and Nobel Prize winner Elie Wiesel was humbling and galvanizing. It wasn't his Holocaust trauma that haunted me; it was his calmness and clarity. He insists on a call to action. His words to me, "Begin anywhere," which I opened my article with, are still strong in my being a decade later. They are always with me.

Wiesel is an author brilliant in his simplicity, a humanitarian, a Holocaust survivor and a modest man. Above all, he's just a man. His shock of black hair, his thin frame, his pale skin, his wrinkles, his self across from myself: they all showed me a human. Just a human carrying forth an urgent story.

I am a person who believes stories are essential. I have staked my life on it—my professional life, my personal core. I have made my living since the day after graduating from SUNY Morrisville telling other people's stories. It is an honor. Some of these stories I have had to dig for, and many I have had to corral from scattered lives and scattered thoughts. I have written about death, horror, illness, transformation, environment, taxes, health and safety, education, murder, and business scams. I have boxes of newspaper and magazine clippings with my byline. Most fulfilling is knowing some of those articles are in *other* people's scrapbooks, and that together, we changed lives.

Wiesel engaged me, and I was in awe of spending time with someone of such profile and accomplishment.

As a writer, I was riveted by "Night," particularly, along with his other books. I was also transfixed by his clear message: "Stop the hate." When he says to pick any cause to help others, when he says a person can make such a difference; he has the right to those words. By passing them along, he gives each of us the right and the weight of those words.

Wiesel evoked candor and quiet. He began writing after being advised to "bear witness," and that is something I hope all writers aspire to. I know I do.

What can you say to a man who lost his mother, sister and father in the night of the Holocaust while most of the world kept silent, scratching itself? You listen, you let him tell his story, and then you do your work to bring that story into the day. Then you make a promise to not only bear witness, but to take action. Words are the first step.

Liza Frenette is the author of three children's novels: "Dangerous Falls Ahead," "Soft Shoulders," and "Dead End." She lives in Albany and is currently the assistant editor for "New York Teacher," a bimonthly publication with a circulation of 575,000.

At age 25, Liza experienced her first "how did I get here" moment when she was flown to New York City from tiny Saranac Lake to attend an awards dinner at Windows on the World at the World Trade Center. She had won first place from United Press International ("exhilarating!") for feature writing based on a Christmas Eve story she had written of a woman whose daughter was missing and later found murdered. Liza has written and taken photographs for weekly and daily newspapers and magazines, including "Reader's Digest."

29

John Glenn to Laura Bush

By Pete Lounsbury
Class of 1976

From my graduation in 1976, I took a continued interest in photography and became the manager of a photography shop in Hudson, NY. From there I moved to Albany, NY where I got involved with a photo store chain called State Photo. All along I honed my photo skills into a portrait business, which moved around the country with me as I explored many avenues and lifestyles.

After becoming a Christian, I continued to use my skills as a photographer in my pilgrim travels. As a 20-something, I lived in Atlanta, Ohio, Wyoming, Oklahoma, New York, New Mexico and Kansas. My two favorite jobs were 1) General photographer and technician under Dr. Grunzig (the inventor of the heart angioplasty procedure at Emory University Hospital) and head photographer at Emporia College in 1986. I began to do wedding photography at this time.

When I got married in 1987, my wife Rose and I settled in Wilmington, DE where we have resided for 20 years. In this time-period, I established Pete Lounsbury Photography and the Brandywine Springs Studio.

As a studio and free-lance photographer, I've photographed about every Senator in Washington, D.C., including Hillary Clinton and Chuck Schumer. I've photographed Laura Bush and countless celebrities, from Brooke Shields to Madeleine Albright. I even spent some time walking with John Glenn, the astronaut, from the Capitol to the Supreme Court building, being chased by a number of school children.

Concerning my time at Morrisville, I fondly remember the times in the darkroom learning to make prints, always being reminded by a joke sign hanging nearby that there was "No smoking, only sex." I remember the school's Pentax Spotmatic I used to learn photojournalism, and Gerald Leone's great instructions which I still apply today. I remember the comradery of the Journalism students and the old typewriters and endless correction tape. I still have copies of the "Wadson and Homes" comic strip I did for *The Chimes* back in 1975-76. I remember Neal Bandlow's praise for my story on parachuting (when I actually jumped out of an airplane at Seneca Falls for The Chimes).

I was proud to be attending one of the finest journalism schools in the country.

I've done very little writing, but have an interesting theological website where my book *The Parable of the Wedding Feast* is in e-book form. My other published book is a children's picture book titled *Jesus and the Blind Man,* currently available at Amazon.com.

I was never interested in getting a bachelor's degree or in any further college. That's why I chose the 2-year associate's degree program. I wanted to get out and start living life. But strangely enough, rarely does a night pass by when I'm not back in Morrisville in my dreams, hanging out with the kids and trying to make the grade. Needless to say, Morrisville made an impression.

Peter Lounsbury can be contacted at Lounsburyus@comcast.net. His business website is www.Lounsbury.us and his personal website is www.withoutthegate.com.

1976

2000

30

Edwin S. Lowe — "Bingo!"

By Timothy Arena
Class of 1975

The most engaging subject I ever interviewed was a businessman who is unknown to most people, but was largely responsible for two of America's best-known forms of entertainment. That man was Edwin S. Lowe, and the forms of entertainment are the games Bingo and Yahtzee.

After Morrisville, I worked for several years as a writer and editor for trade magazines in New York City. One of those magazines was "Toys, Hobbies & Crafts," which covered toy manufacturing and retailing.

While attending a Broadway show, I read a brief article about Edwin S. Lowe, who was then producing a new play on Broadway. According to that article, Lowe made a fortune in the toy and game business, and was poised to make a gamble on Broadway.

Arranging a meeting with Lowe required making dozens of phone calls to his Manhattan office. During an interview he related that in 1929 he was a salesman traveling in rural Georgia when he went to a carnival where people were playing a game called Beano. The game was played with beans and numbered cards, and a winning player yelled out "Beano" and received a Kewpie doll.

Lowe said he returned to New York and played "Beano" with friends. He recalled that one player got so excited after winning she used the word "Bingo" instead of "Beano," and Lowe decided to use that word as the title of his game. He then printed and sold the game, and later hired a mathematician to devise sets of new Bingo cards to allow dozens of people to play and only have one winner.

He said he received a copyright for the game, and eventually it became so popular he sold printing rights, for $1 each, to other companies. He said he sold the rights for a nominal price, against the advice of others, in order to maintain the copyright and meet huge demand for the game. Eventually, the name Bingo entered the public domain.

Lowe also said that in the mid-1950's he was approached by a wealthy couple who created a game played on their yacht, which they called simply, "The Yacht Game." They agreed to let Lowe produce and sell a version of the game.

He said he decided to devise a more marketable name for the game, and dozens of titles were suggested. When someone suggested "Yahtzee" and people laughed, he realized that the laughter actually meant it was a good name for the game.

Sales of "Yahtzee" were very slow at first, he stated, but groups of people who played the game were devoted to it. Lowe then organized "Yahtzee parties" in different cities nationwide, creating word-of-mouth buzz which turned the game into a best seller.

Eventually, he said, he sold the E. S. Lowe Company to Milton Bradley. Years later he used some proceeds of that sale to produce the Broadway play "A Talent for Murder." That play opened soon after the interview, but received unfavorable reviews and closed two months later. Lowe did not produce any more plays, and died in 1986.

Timothy Arena graduated from Morrisville in 1975, and received a BA degree in Communications from SUNY Oswego in 1977. He currently works as an administrator at The New York Times in New York.

Neal Bandlow, Gladys Cleland and Brian McDowell circa 1997

SECTION 4

The First Time You Were Ever Paid

31

A Thrill I'll Never Forget

By Mike Pettinella
Class of 1975

I think it was a story about a very smart parrot. Or maybe it was about a beverage store owner that had an impressive collection of beer cans from all over the world.

In any event, seeing my byline – By Mike Pettinella, Daily News Staff Reporter – for the first time at the top of an article published in a daily newspaper was a thrill I'll never forget. That was in May of 1977, two years after graduating with honors from the Journalism Technology program at Morrisville State College.

Today, 30 years later, I continue to write professionally as a columnist and correspondent for that same newspaper, the *Batavia Daily News*; as a free-lance writer for Genesee Community College, and as a full-time program coordinator/media specialist for Genesee/Orleans Council on Alcoholism and Substance Abuse.

The joy of writing for publication burns as brightly today as it did way back then, when I was a fledging reporter/sports editor/ photographer for my hometown paper. And, without a doubt, my two semesters as a transfer student at Morrisville provided much of what I consider important when it comes to writing.

I enrolled in a 1-plus-1 program at Genesee Community College in Batavia in 1973, knowing that I would be moving to the small Central New York village of Morrisville the following school year. While I was able to earn many credits at Genesee while living at home, I wish I had spent more time at Morrisville.

Morrisville journalism professors Leone, Bandlow, Reeder and Pastore had a profound impact on me. I remember them well. I recall many of the courses and have fond memories of my service to the school newspaper, *The Chimes*.

One of my first assignments was to interview Royson N. Whipple, the school's president. The story was on the front page!

My year at Morrisville flew by. Before I knew it, I was back in Batavia, looking for a job. Thankfully, I didn't have to deliver pizzas or work in convenience stores for long. I landed a position at *The Daily News* and realized my dream as a "professional" journalist.

I worked at *The Daily News* for 15 years, progressing from general assignment reporter to sports editor to assistant news editor. As the police reporter, I covered a murder in Batavia that eventually led to a bank robbery in Las Vegas. As sports editor, I covered the Buffalo Bills and wrote a weekly column. As the assistant news editor, I supervised reporters at the paper's Wyoming County Bureau.

In 1992, I left the newspaper to take a (higher paying) management position. Three years ago, I accepted the program coordinator position at GCASA. At every turn I have used my writing skills to help me succeed.

I have written press releases, created brochures and flyers, produced special sections in the newspaper and have coordinated media coverage of public events. I have been on both sides of the media fence, and have loved every minute of it.

My studies at Genesee reinforced my decision to obtain a journalism degree. My studies at Morrisville poured the foundation for my career – a rock-solid foundation built upon sound principles and practical applications. All I can say is "Thank You" to all my journalism professors at Morrisville and to my fellow students who equally possess a "nose for news" and the desire to express themselves with (AP) style and flair.

Mike is a lifelong resident of Batavia, N.Y., and the program coordinator for the Genesee County Drug-Free Communities Coalition, which was named the national Coalition of the Year for 2006 by Community Anti-Drug Coalitions of America (CADCA). Previously, he was the sports editor and assistant news editor at The Daily News in Batavia and served as general manager of Mancuso Bowling Center, also in Batavia. He continues to write feature stories and a weekly column for the newspaper. He and his wife, Wendy, have four children and four grandchildren. Mike is the current vice president of the Morrisville State College Alumni Board of Directors.

32

It Started With a Paper Route

By David L. Shaw
Class of 1969

It probably started with my paper route, although I wasn't aware of it at the time. Then came Sister Thomas, my English teacher at DeSales High School in Geneva, N.Y. She had us all write a short play. She picked my play about bumbling bank robbers to perform, telling me I had a talent for writing. When it came time to think about college, I remembered Sister Thomas's words. I saw a brochure about a new journalism program starting at a place I'd never heard of, Morrisville.

The program was about writing and newspapers, the only two things I had any interest in at the time. I applied, site unseen, and was accepted (as did probably everyone who applied).

What followed, starting in the fall of 1967, was a two-year journey that set me on a course toward a happy, fulfilling and rewarding 34-year career in print journalism.

The lanky, dark-haired guy in saddle shoes took an uncertain, nervous, quiet young man into a world of passion. Passion for writing and the essential goodness of a free press. Within days, I knew this was the place for me. Journalism according to Jerry Leone saw me learn to construct coherent sentences, to build a news story, paragraph by paragraph. How to write a *lede*. How to write features, hard news and how to be balanced and objective. Take copious notes, he would say before a lecture. Those words served me well in my career.

His passion for the craft was infectious to me. He taught us how to take photos and develop film. We started the *Chimes* and my first by-lined story was an interview of wrestling coach John DeVencenzo.

In addition to teaching the essentials of journalism as it was practiced in that era, Jerry Leone convinced me that journalism was a noble profession, worth pursuing. It worked.

I earned my associate's degree in the first-ever graduating class of 1969. I worked two summers for the newspaper near my hometown. I transferred to West Virginia University and earned an undergraduate degree in journalism in 1971. Vietnam was raging, with Watergate to follow a few years later. Infused with the skills I learned from Jerry, and others at WVU, my career began. I was hired as sports editor/reporter for a very small daily in the spring of 1972. It paid $98 a week and the paper folded nine months later.

The experience of being a one-person sports department was often overwhelming. Could Jerry have been wrong? Of course not. The AP guy who serviced that tiny paper recommended me to the Syracuse Newspapers. I began in August 1973 and literally thousands of by-lines later, I retired May 31, 2007. I began working part-time for the Geneva newspaper July 2. I believe I was respected as a solid, fair, thorough journalist. Jerry taught me well.

Thanks to Jerry Leone's impact, I can honestly say I have earned a living in the best way possible. I looked forward to going to work every day. It turned out just as Jerry said it could. I owe him a tremendous debt. I was fortunate he was a part of my life.

David worked for the Wayne County Star from 1972-1973 before settling in for a long run with the Syracuse Post-Standard from 1973-2007. He is spending his "retirement time" with the Finger Lakes Times.

33

When A Detour Is A Good Thing...

By Matt Amodeo

Class of 1979

High school was in the rear-view mirror and I was headed west to visit a few colleges. We decided to take a "detour" and shoot down to the "two-year" school before our appointment later in the day at the "four-year" school.

Upon entering the building housing the Journalism offices, we heard spirited conversation echoing through the empty halls. An aspiring sports writer – I had been covering high school sports as a stringer for a local Gannett daily – I immediately picked up on the sports banter growing louder as we approached the instructor's office.

As I poked my head in to make introductions, I saw an animated blond-haired professor gesturing wildly from his chair while making some remarks about the Detroit Tigers (or was it Michigan State?!) as several students standing around him rolled their eyes and waved him off laughingly.

I often tell friends that if Morrisville had been a four-year college, I never would have transferred to College Park, Maryland.

Don't get me wrong – I have enjoyed a wonderful experience here in the Washington area, where I have lived and worked for more than 27 years. But the educational relationships and experience were hands-down superior at Morrisville.

And the friendships with many Morrisville grads continue to this day.

We never made that afternoon appointment.

Matt Amodeo is the owner/president of Publicity Matters, a Washington DC-based public relations firm representing national and international clients for the last 25 years.

Brian McDowell, Mary Ellen Mengucci and Neal Bandlow

34

Launching *Dog Days of Denver*

By Kim Jackson
Class of 1978

I got the first dog of my life in 1998. I quickly learned about the underground world of people and their dogs, where everyone knows your dog's name and everything about him, but not you or your name. And it's okay, almost preferable. It was a new experience for me and I was content to explore this new life with my dog.

One day, I thought it'd be nice to have a magazine about what's going on in the world of dogs in Denver. Having published client business-to-business customer and professional association newsletters, I knew I could do it. But was there a market for it? I started collecting information to find out.

In early 2001, I commissioned a research firm to check out the viability of a dog magazine in Denver. The president of the company personally called and said, "If you don't do this, someone else will."

So I did. Within a couple of hours, I had a complete 18-month editorial calendar. A Canadian publisher friend, who had launched successful national titles, helped me with a rate sheet. I got a mock-up of the template made and started selling advertising.

Within six weeks of deciding to publish, *Dog Days of Denver* was launched at the metro area's largest animal fundraising event — The Furry Scurry — where 10,000 people walk the two-mile loop around a park with their dogs. The bimonthly magazine became an instant hit.

As editor, I interviewed people, wrote stories and took photos. One day I realized with a start that I was FINALLY doing journalism. No more company messages hidden inside a newsletter article. No more annual reports or brochures. Journalism. And my mind instantly shot back to the days in the *Chimes* office, where Matt Amodeo, Steve Michaud and I would decide which stories would make the page and who'd get a byline. Like in the *Chimes* office, I felt more alive and invigorated with *Dog Days* than I had in a very long time.

After the first couple of issues, I discovered my voice. My writing grew stronger, because of my passion and my interest in the topic. And I didn't hold back as I had done with writing for clients. All that I had learned at Morrisville was made good with *Dog Days*: the writing and editing, photography, graphics of communications, even Charlie Hammond's advertising and PR classes. What I learned at Morrisville—in classes and through my experience as associate editor at the *Chimes*—along with my Business Administration degree and career experience, culminated in a magazine that was met with overwhelming response.

My passion was contagious. Friends and business associates distributed the magazine. Non-profit organizations readily signed up to receive a portion of each subscription as a donation, in exchange for distributing *Dog Days* to their supporters. Somewhere along the line, people began to think I was an expert on dogs, and I became a regular guest on two radio stations.

One day, after two years of nearly non-stop work, I hit the wall and slid to the floor, like a cartoon character. It was simply over, and I pulled the plug. Four years later, people in the industry—and dog lovers who remember it— still approach me about getting the magazine started again.

Instead, I now enjoy my dogs—rather than talk about enjoying them. And while I still see another dog-related story in the making nearly every day, I'm content these days to just take walks with my own dogs.

...Or am I?

Kim Jackson lives in Denver. She is pictured with her two dogs, Simba and Saasha. Sadly, Saasha, the Alaskan Malamute on the right, died of lymphoma in late September 2007. In business for 14 years, Kim specializes in custom publishing magazines for clients. She and Simba can often be found out and about in Denver or up in the Rocky Mountains, exploring new territory—both real and imagined.

35

Heat & Marlins Broadcast TV Launch

By Karen Rickard
Class of 1974

Not too many years ago, just before dawn, I was driving to my job on Miami Beach. It was my custom to arrive early on South Beach, since almost everyone else arrives late and stays even later, or is that earlier? As I was heading south on the less than crowded I-95, the dawning sun was illuminating the caravan of overseas flights that arrive at Miami International Airport in the early morning hours. They stacked up in a line stretching far toward the eastern horizon. The highway undulated before me, dipping down and then raising for each overpass. Almost in unison with the undulations were the huge jets crossing the plane of the highway on their final approach to MIA.

As I came to the interchange that was my turn to Miami Beach, a most unique and familiar nose came into view over the highway. The down turned nose-cone could be only one plane; it was the supersonic Concorde arriving on its weekly run from London. It instantly captured me and I slowed to observe the high speed bird that seemed to be gliding to the ground. The passengers had come so far, embarking in London, sleeping through the night, to awaken half a world away. Surely this was the jet-set that would bake on the beach shortly and then party late into the night at the South Beach clubs.

As I made the eastward turn, the raising sun was full in my eyes, and I reflected on how far I had come. To quote the Grateful Dead, "what a long strange trip" it had been for a girl from Poland, New York to be working in Miami. There was no doubt what had steered me so far from a small town in central New York; it was the journalism program at Morrisville.

The guidance of those men, Leone, Bandlow, Hammond, Reeder, had opened my eyes to so many amazing things. I left Morrisville sure that I could tackle anything I wanted to do. I had learned far more then how to write a news story; and I had grown far beyond anything I could have imagined.

The foundation of the J-program at Morrisville had allowed me to launch both Miami Heat NBA Basketball and Florida Marlins Major League Baseball, as executive producer for their first over-the-air television broadcasts. I approached sports production with the same curiosity that a good journalist uses to get the most information from his sources. That was just a small part of the continual personal re-invention that put me on the highway that magical morning in Miami.

I remain certain in the conviction that Morrisville taught me to reach out and grasp every new opportunity. The wonderful relationships that existed between and among students and instructors helped forge my ability to create lasting relationships with colleagues and superiors. Most people would believe that my adventures over the last 20 years have been the most memorable and exciting of my life. However, those years would only be the end result of the most rewarding two years of my life; my years at Morrisville.

36

Publishing Soft Porn for Women?

By Leslie Roman-Williams
Class of 1973

I recall vividly my first visit to Morrisville as a high-school senior. My parents had driven me the four hours from Dunkirk to see how I might like being enrolled in what was then (1971) one of the few Journalism programs in the state. I remember seeing Jerry Leone in classroom action, all energy and enthusiasm; dark eyes twinkling and arms akimbo, making some important point.

Thirty-six years later, I am still smiling at the memories.

We of the Class of 1973 typed our stories on clunky manual machines, snapped photos with unwieldy but expensive cameras, and hit the local radio airwaves with our brand of cool...or what passed for it in that era.

Some of our professors were colorful (those my classmates will not forget) but ones like Charlie Hammond, guru of advertising and public relations, were scrupulously professional, objective, and inspiring.

After graduation and a four-month job search in London, England (the energy crisis and IRA bomb scares made it a lonely and dangerous place) I moved to Chicago, where I suspect I was one of few Mo'ville grads ever to be hired immediately as managing editor at a soft-porn magazine targeted for females. (FOXYLADY, a ripoff of PLAYGIRL). My innocence was superseded by my ignorance of the magazine's shady owners, who may have been using the magazine as a front. Mobsters? I never knew for sure, but my name and title looked swell in print and my friends and family thought the whole thing was impressive, if a little— well, very—peculiar.

Not surprisingly, the magazine folded in less than two years.

FAST FORWARD to 1998 when, after a career with Hyatt Hotels, I decided moving around the country and working killer hours had lost their charms, I took a job as proofreader, then copywriter, with the Richmond Times-Dispatch. I tell people jokingly that I get paid to write all those advertising lies for a living, but of course, that is untrue. I help inform readers about products and services—not a bad thing—and I contribute articles weekly about trends for our Homes page, plus write for special sections.

From 2003-2006 my husband and I took to the roads of America, Canada, and Mexico in a roadside ministry and ended up writing a book about our spiritual and motoring journeys titled, "Altar Mobile: We Brake for Faith," published in December 2005 by Publish America.

How did I get here? Who really knows?...but as Oprah writes monthly, "this I know for sure": one of the earliest stops was at Morrisville.

Thanks, Jerry Leone, for the ticket to lots of adventures.

Leslie Roman-Williams lives in Richmond, VA.

37

24 Years of Editorial Cartoons

By Thom Zajac
Class of 1975

I broke my collarbone sliding down an icy mound at Morrisville the first time it snowed my freshman year. During my senior year, I wrote a weekly political column for *The Chimes*. I graduated in 1975 and moved to northern California shortly thereafter.

When I look back at my years at Morrisville, I do so fondly, though I am now certain I did not fully appreciate it at the time.

Here's my journalism story.

It took me a while to find the profession that attracted me most: editorial cartooning. This presented a significant challenge for me, as I didn't know the first thing about drawing. I wish I could tell you that I mastered the craft quickly, became editorial cartoonist for The San Francisco Chronicle, and then went on to great fame; but that's not what happened.

Something funny happened. An epiphany, actually.

In a moment of great excitement, I saw that in this troubled world there existed a plethora of Pulitzer-prize winning editorial cartoonists—dozens of them. Each of them drew nearly a cartoon a day, and most newspapers carried only one or maybe two of these splendid things. And printing all the good ones would be a powerful and compelling presentation of the news. It became absolutely clear to me that I wasn't destined to become an editorial cartoonist; I was destined to exploit them. In a good way, of course. As a publisher.

The first issue of *The Santa Cruz Comic News* hit the streets September 12, 1984, when Reagan was running for reelection against Mondale. It did not go unnoticed; over the course of the next ten years, *The Santa Cruz Comic News* would inspire the creation of over 75 'comic newspapers' nationwide and a few abroad as well. Many of these publications have long gone by the wayside, but The *Comic News* is still going strong here in 2007. And with a little luck and due diligence, our Web site (http://www.thecomicnews.com) will soon become a national player in the 'liberal blogosphere'.

It's been an interesting career. I think it's possible that I've looked at more editorial cartoons over the past 24 years than anyone on earth. When they are terrific, they show a perspective that simply cannot be attained in any other way. Put a few of these terrific efforts together, and the power, I think, is astounding.

But that's just my opinion.

Lastly, a warm thanks to Neal Bandlow, Dan Reeder, and Jerry Leone for sharing your tremendous enthusiasm for newspaper journalism. You have inspired us all.

Thom Zajac lives in Santa Cruz, CA.

38

From Student to Instructor at Buffalo

By Aaron Gifford
Class of 1992

When I left Morrisville State College in May of 1992, I never dreamed I'd return to Madison County. But indeed, I came back. Twice.

I can't even begin to detail the wealth of knowledge I acquired during my two years at SUNY Morrisville in both journalism career training and personal growth. But I can say that the most valuable piece of advice came from Neal Bandlow.

He told us not to be afraid to major in something other than journalism when we transferred. I was so moved by what I learned in Jean Gosling's sociology and urban sociology courses at Morrisville that I decided to further my interest in that subject at the University of Buffalo. I continued my interest in reporting by writing for the student-run *Spectrum*, which came out three times a week.

Editors at the Spectrum told me that my journalism training was way beyond anything that was offered in UB's communication or English programs, so they asked me to instruct other staff writers at the Spectrum. It was a humbling experience for me, because so many of these students were academic stars in high school and went to UB for some of its nationally-acclaimed programs; yet they wanted to learn from me and were starving for any second-hand wisdom I could pass on from my two-year alma mater.

After graduation, I was hired at the Oneida Daily Dispatch in Madison County. I was responsible for turning over at least two stories a day. My first byline was a story from the 7 a.m. Oneida City Hospital Board of Managers meeting. I was able to file the story for the same day's paper. Indeed, those timed news-writing lab drills at Morrisville had paid off.

I spent two years at the Watertown Daily Times, where I mainly covered the Akwesasne Mohawk reservation. It was there where I first discovered that my sociology background came in handy on so many different levels.

After years of trying to get in the door, the Post-Standard finally hired me in 1999. I worked in the Oswego County bureau for a year and then moved to the Madison County office, where I still am today.

In covering crime, small-town happenings and rural poverty issues, not a day goes by when I don't stop to reflect on the basic guidelines of journalism I learned at Morrisville and the sociological perspectives I gained there and at UB.

I never did get a chance to thank Neal for that advice. And I take back any snickers I may have made when Jerry, Pam and Mary Ellen assured us that Madison County ain't such a bad place.

Aaron Gifford lives in Cazenovia and has been a full-time newspaper reporter since 1995. He works for the Syracuse Post Standard and has aspirations of being a columnist or international correspondent for a major metro daily.

39

Moment of Fame in Cooperstown

By Betsy Wilcox
Class of 1996

My life has taken a lot of twists and turns since I graduated from the SUNY Morrisville Journalism program in 1996. So many turns, in fact, I am not even employed by a newspaper, online publication or radio or television station any more. Somehow, I managed to get into academia (who'd have thunk that?!).

However, for a brief shining moment, I WAS a reporter.

I'll never forget the first time I saw my name in print in a real newspaper. I was working for a weekly in upstate New York, The Coopers-Town Crier.

What a thrill! I got to go by the Baseball Hall of Fame every day on my short walk to work. God, I felt so important! Granted, my job was only that of a part-time news clerk, but, hey, I was working and loving every minute of it.

My good fortune at having an article published (on the front page, no less!) came just one day after the Independence Day celebrations in downtown Cooperstown. There was a terribly frightening incident at the park where the fireworks display was to take place. A young man parked his car on an incline, but forgot to engage his emergency brake and the car decided it didn't want to sit still. It rolled backward down the hill and managed to hit three people before slamming into a tree. When I got to work the next morning, I was telling my editor about the incident. He said to me, "you're an eyewitness. Why don't you take the story?" You could have knocked me over with a feather!

I immediately jumped on the horn and began doing interviews. The final piece I ended up with wasn't great, but with some help from my editor, we turned it into a printable story. The next edition that was to be published had my name and byline—above the fold, even!

It wasn't an isolated event, either. My editor was slowing giving me more and more responsibilities. I might have even stuck with it, had I not been given an opportunity to work at a daily just up the road in Oneonta. I decided to take the position because it offered me full-time hours.

However, my clerical duties were increased at the new job, so I never got another chance at reporting. Its never bothered me, though. I had my moment in the sun, and the few months I worked at the Crier are some of my fondest memories ever.

Thanks, Mr. Gates, for being such a great editor.

And thanks especially, Neal, Jerry, Brian and Mary Ellen, for giving me the skills and tools I needed. I love you all!

Betsy Wilcox has held many different jobs in a variety of business and professional offices, including a law firm, a state hospital and a not-for-profit foundation. She currently works for the Vestal School District in Vestal, NY as a secretary in the high school guidance office. She lives in Endicott, NY with her husband and her two sons.

40

Amsterdam's 1st Female Beat Reporter

By Joanne Guilmette
Class of 1971

As the daughter of a newspaper printer with printer's ink in my veins, journalism has been my passion for as long as I can remember.

Some of my earliest memories involve my dad showing me the large linotype machines in the dirty, dingy composing room that today's journalism students would not recognize. As a teenager growing up in the 60's, I constantly played broadcast TV pioneer Nancy Dickerson by interviewing my sister, whom I called "Jackie Kennedy."

But my career plans changed when my parents could only afford a two-year college and a guidance counselor convinced me I would never get a newspaper job with an associate's degree. My English teacher, who had moved out of state, returned for my graduation and wrote an inspirational message in my yearbook that convinced me I had to pursue a journalism career. A senior journalism student at Morrisville—and son of my dad's newspaper colleague—took me directly to see Jerry Leone on my first day at Morrisville, and I was able to quickly switch my major to journalism.

One of my fondest memories was interviewing and hanging out behind stage with the "Vogues," a nationally popular musical group of the 60's. One of them said "honey, do you have a cigarette?" It was the only time in my life I regretted not being a smoker.

It took a year before I landed my first journalism job during the post-Watergate years, when everyone wanted to be the next Bob Woodward. I worked for a weekly Jewish newspaper, writing about Bar Mitzvahs. Cockroaches were my daily companions.

Soon I landed my first job at a small daily newspaper and became the "society editor." When the job of education reporter opened up, I asked to be considered. It was the early 70's and a female had never worked as a beat reporter there. But the editor told me I could try out by performing both jobs at once. The workload was overwhelming, but I passed with flying colors and soon became the first female beat reporter. After that a married colleague, who later became an assistant to the governor, became angry that I continually refused his advances and tried to get me fired.

I managed to hang on. I interviewed the very colorful former Congresswoman Bella Abzug and was dying to know why she always wore her signature big hats. "So that I wouldn't be mistaken for a secretary" in the days when female lawyers were still a rarity, she said.

I moved to a larger paper. There, as a police reporter, I covered a major bridge collapse. My heart raced as I ran to the scene, not knowing what awaited me, but I quickly collared the key witnesses. We won an AP award.

As the Albany County reporter, I worked for months—without the encouragement of my editors—filing freedom of information requests to get the name of a nurse anesthetist. She had been on duty when a 30-year -old patient mysteriously went into a coma and died after emergency surgery at Albany Medical Center on Thanksgiving Day. I tracked the nurse down to an out-of-state address, and she told me she had been a student, working without supervision that day, since there were never anesthesiologists on duty on holidays. When my story appeared—contradicting the story of the hospital spokesman—the policy was changed to ensure an anesthesiologist was always on duty—even on holidays.

Later, I was named business editor. The ad director tried to get me fired when I refused to confine my Sunday profiles to his advertising clients as my predecessor had. The journalistic ethics I had learned at Morrisville would not allow me to compromise. I totally revamped the business pages, and soon the same advertisers were clamoring to be in the business section. I won two more AP awards.

I worked for 15 years as a journalist, and it was an amazing career for someone with an associate degree. For the past 20 years I have repeatedly called upon my experience as a journalist to forge a very successful career on the "other side" in public relations. Working now in an environment where many have doctorates, I recently told my boss—also a PHD—that I should probably go back to college to get at least a bachelor's degree so I could move ahead. "Why bother?" he said. "You're doing great!"

Joanne worked at the Amsterdam Evening Recorder and became the newspaper's first female beat reporter in 1974. She won three AP awards while at the Troy Record. Since 2001 she has been the director of media relations at the New York State Museum.

41

Back to the Future Curriculum?

By Andrew Goldberger
Class of 1996

In 1989, at 13 years old, I began publishing a newsletter about my first love, professional wrestling. I used money from 200 monthly subscribers to buy Aldus Pagemaker software for my Macintosh computer, added a laser printer, a bit too much clip art, and the occasional scanned photo of a bloodied wrestler. Five long years later, having escaped my short-lived love affair with pro wrestling, I found my way to "Mo'ville" with a few missions to accomplish: learn the craft of journalism, catapult myself into a career of reporting the news, and have a few more short-lived love affairs.

1994-1996 was a great time for technical innovators in Morrisville and in the world of journalism. The Internet was in its infancy, the O.J. trial had begun, and a team of television journalists brought unprecedented access to our legal system. The DVD format was announced. Yet Charlton Hall still had scarred lightboards, boxes of prickly X-acto knives, and a photolab that reeked of chemicals. Those were the smells, sights, and feel of old-school journalism. Our professors were "throwbacks."

Don't mistake the primitive technology for budget cuts or Luddism. Whether our fearless leaders knew it or not, they forced bratty self-centered Long Island Jewish kids and their cow-milking brethren from upstate to have a foundation of theory first, followed by layers of old-school practice, so as to establish that we weren't walking into the newsrooms of tomorrow without a healthy appreciation for the newsrooms of yesteryear.

We learned old-school layout and design with long strips of news articles, lining up layout margin lines with lines of copy, and using a small blade to crop the article to fit (adding leading), sometimes line by line. It was a tedious process. It was messy. Frequently, my finger would get pricked. I bled for this process.

Consistently, my layouts would've been much cleaner and more aligned with the use of a computer layout program. Thankfully, there were no shortcuts in our beloved Journalism program. Currently, in my company's graphic design department, I see a young designer using Adobe Illustrator or Quark Xpress or Adobe Photoshop. I see digital tools from the toolbar called "crop" "measure" and "slice." I see "leading" and "kerning." Most designers born in 1976 or after have never experienced the first-hand usage of these tools, and will forever think they are simply quirkily-named.

The class of '96 was the last to use manual paste-up at Morrisville.

Neal Bandlow was gracious enough to present me a 1-course-credit opportunity to summarize all of the tools needed to create an electronic newsroom, incorporating Aldus Pagemaker in its newer form (Adobe Pagemaker) and scanning into the weekly *Chimes* process. I used everything I learned from my teen years as a computer-based newsletter designer. Today, Pagemaker isn't relevant to my professional life, but the foundation of journalism—the "why" behind the "what"—still is. To add context. To help people understand. To tell a compelling story. And to understand that today's innovations aren't possible without yesterday's sacrifices.

I remember Day 1 in Newswriting class. "The '30' at the end of every news story, we write '30' class. That gives the typesetter an instruction so that they'll know the story is over and that they'll stop printing." Today's newsroom workers don't need to use "30", but don't they need to know? Upon further research, "30" is believed to be used because in the "hot lead" printing era, "30" was the cue for the typesetter to insert a 30-point slugline as spacing between the end of one story and beginning of the next headline. Others believe it was telegraph shorthand for "End." This practice is obviously devoid of any value in the digital age. But respect and knowledge of its meaning adds depth and context to our understanding of our roots.

My good friend runs a division of the New York Times called "Times Select." The business plan of that unit states that it is possible (and probable), that the printed newspaper is a thing of the past. That all of our news, soon enough, will be digitally distributed. The evolution of print journalism is nothing to shy away from. As someone who makes his living off of the digitization of archaic processes, I only pause briefly in hesitation before welcoming the electronic age of journalism. The journalists of tomorrow ought to recognize the path that brought them there. Someone will remember their carpal tunnel as we will remember our X-acto-knife cuts.

My Pagemaker skills didn't noticeably improve in Morrisville. The context did. And, as all journalists know, context is everything.

42

Getting the Presidential Treatment

By Tom Lemery
Class of 1986

I'm sure there are "must-have" memories in this book. If there were not, then you would be sorry they weren't included. I know at least one person would be disappointed if I didn't write this. I hope you enjoy this memory as much as Neal (Bandlow) and I do.

In the fall of 1985, I was an Individual Studies student at the college... a "J-wannabe," if you will... All the journalism students were in every other seat in alphabetical order. I was sitting in the last row with other "J-wannabes" in one of the big lecture halls in the Lab Classroom Building (now called Crawford Hall).

One day, our class was learning about press conferences. In this exercise, there was a list of questions that Neal handed out to us. We had to raise our hand, stand up, state our name and newspaper, then ask the question. There were five people, including myself, asked by Neal to be the "reporters" in the class. So we "practiced" as Neal was the spokesperson.

One by one, each student raised their hands, stated their names and newspaper, then recited the question they were asked to read. Neal would call on these reporters and answer the questions as any good spokesperson would....then it was my turn.

I raised my hand. Neal sees me, points, and says, "Let's hear from the tall and lanky dummy in the back who thinks he knows anything about soccer."

As the class was chuckling, I stand up, and with my best Ronald Reagan voice, I say, "Ronald Reagan, White House News." This brought a bigger laugh from the class...and Neal too. Then I asked my question as Reagan.

When it was all said and done, the class enjoyed this exchange, and clapped.

Tom Lemery practices community journalism in Morrisville, including a local weekly column about Morrisville village happenings. He remains close to the college, having delighted audiences as a featured performer in many Friars' Club theatrical productions. His work as announcer at college sporting events continues to this day.

Journalism faculty and their spouses in 1979.

SECTION 5

And Now, a Word about the Professors

43

Bandlow: 27 Years of High-Octane

By Brian L. McDowell, Assistant Professor
Reprinted from The Morrisville Chimes, September 1999

One of my many lasting memories of Neal Bandlow is seeing him walk down the hall, a battered, overfilled cardboard box in hand, on his way to lead another freshman lecture.

The man clearly never understood the need for a briefcase.

Neal Bandlow was always moving, always smiling, always listening and always talking. Nobody I have known ever outworked him. His students knew him as the one person who was always happy to see them. His colleagues knew him as a good friend, a brilliant lecturer, a born teacher.

Twenty-seven years after he came to Morrisville "to teach for a few years," Neal made the hardest decision of his life in June when he finally agreed to the wishes of his wife, Carol, and returned to the Detroit area his parents and other family members call home.

For his more than 1,300 former students, he remains a trusted counsel, a loyal friend, an unabashed cheerleader of their successes now and for the rest of their lives.

Preparing for this weekend's alumni reception for Neal, I was struck by the consistency in the hundreds of alumni messages that poured in for him: class of 73; class of 98; it makes no difference. The message reads the same:

You touched my life at a time when I needed it the most.
You helped me become what I am.
You accepted me without reservation, without condition.
You believed in me... before I believed in myself.
You made learning fun.

A wise man once said that a good teacher never knows where his influence will stop. Neal Bandlow was—and remains—a very good teacher. Luckily he has youth of spirit, good health, and decades ahead when he will have the opportunity to read and hear all about his influence in the lives of his former students.

Yet I have no doubt that this man whom I still introduce as the best lecturer I have ever known, this war veteran who has spoken reluctantly in low, almost reverent tones to unknowing teenagers about unthinkable horrors that brought him home from Vietnam with lifelong wounds and two purple hearts, this educator who always was learning and never stopped giving, will take little credit for his students' successes.

"Oh, hey," I can almost hear him saying in that trademark loud baritone, his hands wildly waving: "It was always them. They just needed to believe in themselves."

This column wouldn't look right on page 2, the Editorials page. Neal certainly would never have allowed it there during his 18 years as CHIMES advisor. I chose page 6 because that has always been the 'jumps' page, where 'continued' stories have their end, the last page to be finished in each issue.

Neal's is an ongoing story of his great loyalty to this college and his great delight in the details of former students' lives beyond Morrisville.

As he reaches the end of his teaching story, I and all of Neal Bandlow's other friends can take equal joy in the word at the bottom of this last column:

'Continued…'

If Jerry Leone was the "Denny McClain" of the Journalism staff, then Neal was certainly the "Mickey Lolich". For 27 years, he remained one of the most dynamic professors in the school's history. In 1999, he earned the equivalent of a "Hall of Fame" induction when he was awarded Morrisville's "Distinguished Faculty Award."

44

Working in a Cutting-Edge Environment

By Patricia Swann

Assistant Professor of Journalism, 1999-2002

My time spent as assistant professor of journalism at SUNY Morris-ville from 1999-2002 laid the groundwork for my research and publication work today. I am currently associate professor of public relations at Utica College. I have recently published a textbook of case studies in public relations management.

Cases in Public Relations Management looks at all areas of strategic communication strategy including crisis communication management, media, consumer, employee and community, international, governmental and financial relations. The book discusses different types of examples, some with outcomes that were not always successful, to teach readers to approach situations analytically. The textbook is intended for communi-cation professionals and upper-level public relations students and was published by McGraw-Hill.

Some of the case studies examined the military and government's response to the Abu Ghraib Iraqi prisoner abuse scandal, Kansas' brand-ing campaign, Hallmark's listening and promotional tour.

In addition to the textbook, I conduct research and speak on school district Web sites and on Internet technology's effects on organizational communication.

Morrisville College has played an important role in my career as a teacher. It was my first teaching job and that three-year experience taught me the importance of teaching students through applied learning. Some of my favorite memories included working with students in the photo darkroom labs (with music playing loudly). One year students did a photo show that depicted a "day in the life" of the town of Morrisville. I also have good memories of working with The Chimes photo staff. I remem-ber the great job students did of covering 9/11's impact from the campus perspective. I also remember the laptops and how amazing it was to work in a cutting-edge educational environment. Brian McDowell's famous impersonations always made me laugh. His drive to help students succeed was a wonder to behold. Brian was a great role model for me as a beginning teacher; he also was and *is* a great friend!

Congratulations to Morrisville College's superb journalism program...and good luck with your next 40 years!

Pat Swann spent her first three years as a college professor at Morrisville State. She now teaches in the Public relations Department at Utica College. She is missed on a daily basis by the faculty who worked with her.

45

Precious Memories of Mo'Ville

By Dan Reeder

Professor of Journalism, 1973-1976

My Introduction

I flew into Syracuse for the job interview, expecting "saddle-shoes" Leone to meet me. Instead, he played golf and sent Neal, telling him to look for a "tall, blond guy." Neal and I circled each other for half an hour before we finally figured it out. By the time we got to Mo'ville, we'd bonded, and the chaos was launched. Leone had started the relationship with a practical joke - just the encouragement Bandlow and I needed! We became the three musketeers, swashbuckling across campus en route to our next adventure. Our wives became close friends, too, and the six of us were nearly inseparable. [Jerry started the program the year I graduated from high school. This saga began six years after that.]

The Work

Mostly what I remember was the incredible work load. Because I was a greenhorn, I faced having to create lectures and labs one step ahead of delivering them. Even in the third year, I was still creating lectures for courses I hadn't yet taught. One reason for the incessant work was a heavy teaching load, but the other reason was the large enrollment.

This was post-Watergate, remember, and all the journalism programs were flooded with majors wanting to be Woodward and Bernstein. Reporters on The Chimes found administration conspiracies around every corner. It was a heady time to study – and to teach – journalism. The program grew to five full-time faculty members in fewer than 10 years.

Colleagues

From journalism: Jerry, Neal, Charlie, Art, Ann, Doris [!]; Dave from sociology and John from poli-sci; Bert and Dave from hotel management; Frank and Tami and Kate from student affairs, or whatever it was; Mark Jones, from math; and Division Chair Larry Baker ("What are we going to do with you and Bandlow?"); Roy Whipple and John Stewart and all the coaches.

school bus behind his house, about 12 feet from where we slept. Every winter morning – including Saturdays! – we were awakened at about 6 a.m. when he started that bus. Ten consecutive minutes of revving and popping. He is lucky to have died of natural causes.

Students

I cannot possibly mention you all, but I can muster a mental image of about 95 percent of you – still frozen as you were at 20 or 21. I was only five or six years older than most of you. So how is it that you've stayed young and I've grown old?

I have great memories of all of my Chimes editors, a talented and courageous lot. Ed and Zonker, Mike S., Karen Budzynski (I even eventually learned to pronounce it!), Steve Cirello, Dave Snyder and Martin and Casey. There were many more. Remember the production treks to Chittenango? [The computer was still 10 years away, practically speaking.] Wax machines and trimmed galleys and re-written heads to fit. All that additional labor! Giving up all those Sundays! It really is easier today, huh?

Nancy Cardillo swears that I committed a vulgar act during an editing lecture on the difference between "hanged" and "hung." I think she made it up.

In a course called "Specialized Writing," I lectured for one hour a week, and the remaining two hours (plus several more) were devoted to 20-minute "tutorials" with each student. During this time, we reviewed the student's writing assignment, which was usually bleeding with red ink. One particular student, David Chartock, had the particularly annoying habit of arguing with me about grammar and style, none of which rules I had created. I quickly got to the point of kicking him out of my office when he started that nonsense. [Professors Neal and Dave and John, in adjacent offices, would make bets on how long it would take for Chartock to get kicked out this week.] David had the last laugh. He won the New York State Editorial Writing contest that year at St. Bonaventure. No hard feelings, David.

Crazy Bob Fenner came to a Christmas party at our house and broke a dining room chair. Thing just exploded. One of the funnier sights I've ever seen.

Big Jim, who insisted that my drink order really should be "Scotch *plus* water." As I recall, one of those drinks at the Town House at the time cost ninety cents. ... Deb K. and I singing with the juke box songs ... Bar arguments about politics, sports, religion, sex, the meaning of life and why I was such an s.o.b. in the classroom. [Confession: We had only two years to get you ready.]

Neal

Most of what is really interesting will have to wait for my book. We would teach like crazy all day and then spend two hours talking on the phone at night … greasy eggs at 2:30 in the morning at some all-night joint on Route 20 … buying drinks for 18-year-olds at the Town House (before the age limit changed) … Neal and I dodging the campus security as we whizzed across the campus in his Honda Civic in the middle of the night … spending one glorious summer playing tennis and another tending a garden the size of Rhode Island … cold snowy weekend nights when Carol and Janet would go home at midnight and Neal would get me home about 3, climbing on top of the old Chevy to announce to the world that "He's home, May. The drunk sonofabitch is finally home!" … terrific, raucous times with his Michigan State buddies who would visit … Friday nights at the all-you-could-eat fried fish place near Eaton … faculty parties where we'd try to get Charlie Hammond drunk … great parties at Jerry & Barb's … disco dancing in Syracuse (well, Neal and Big Jer never danced much, but Carol and Barb and Janet and I did, wearing that hideous double-knit…) … lunches at STUAC with Frank and the boys.

…. The pain of leaving to return to Kansas. I remember that as if it were yesterday.

Not That It Matters

The quick summary since the summer of '76: I edited Kansas Alumni periodicals for nine years while I also occasionally taught at the KU School of Journalism, and then launched Reeder & Co., which I still operate. We're a creative firm specializing in graphic design, advertising and editorial services. Higher education is our primary, though not exclusive, niche. I travel quite a bit and have served some 40 colleges and universities variously. I also have a stake in ReederVogel Advertising in San Antonio, where I occasionally show up and cause trouble. My folks are in charge there, but I may have to take over some day.

Janet will retire at the end of the '08 school year from her long-held job as "library media specialist" [read: elementary librarian] and we are seriously considering moving to the Hill Country of Texas. Our son, Tim, 27, lives in Austin, and I have a brother nearby in Fredericksburg.

I can't retire for another couple or three years [shut up, Bandlow], but I wouldn't mind finding something else to do when we change scenery. Truth is, it ain't likely. Old dogs/new tricks theory.

We've loved living in Lawrence, where basketball reigns and football still sucks. But it may be time for a change while we're still physically ablc!

103

And Finally …

I have wonderful, precious memories of our three years at Mo'ville. That short time was enormously rewarding for me personally and professionally. Of course, I have each of my students to thank for that, as well as top-shelf colleagues. Neal and Carol and Jerry and Barb are lifelong friends.

I would appreciate and enjoy hearing from you, and I send both gratitude and affection your way. Congratulations to the Morrisville State journalism program for reaching its 40th birthday.

The Kansas Jayhawks entered a Nov. 24 contest with Missouri as the second-ranked college football team in the country. They lost, but their record fell to a still-impressive 11-1. So much for 'old dogs', Dan?

**Dan Reeder, 1609 Alvamar Drive, Lawrence, KS 66047
785.842.2383   reeder@sunflower.com**

Dan Reeder in 1976

46

The Lucky One

By Mary Ellen Mengucci
Assistant Professor of Journalism, 1991-1996

I taught in this remarkable, one-of-a-kind program for *five* wonderful years, starting in 1991. I was "LUCKY" enough to join the J-faculty during the era of the "Old-Boys' Club," when many of the key players were still here: Jerry Leone as innovative program founder and department chair; Neal Bandlow as passionate news teacher and *Chimes* advisor; and Brian McDowell, who at that time ran the PR office on campus and dedicated himself to helping us teach our newswriting labs.

I was "LUCKY", too, that my years here in the early 1990s coincided with an almost magical era in the J-program:

•Our enrollment numbers soared: over 115 kids in the freshman Journalism class *alone* the year I started.

•Cash flowed—as much as it ever did—in the State University of New York.

•Our dean, Greg Gray, was wise enough to know we were a unique program—a family, really—and he graciously supported us, even if he didn't always understand us.

•Our labs underwent full computerization and internet connections.

•And we managed to move WCVM Radio from the subterranean dregs of a dormitory to its current location in Charlton Hall.

Every day I was "LUCKY" enough to work with the unlikeliest, yet thoroughly entertaining cast of characters you could *never* imagine:

First, I worked with an old guy wearing saddle shoes, who had but eight toes on his two feet, who told corny, corny jokes, who couldn't remember a student's name to save his life, and who provided me with a lifetime of fodder by regularly taking me with him to the Shamrock Inn for lunch with the nicest, but quirkiest bunch of old codgers you'll ever meet.

Second, I worked with a Vietnam vet who had less hair and less socks than the rest of us, but more boxes of overhead lecture notes, more folders crammed with handouts, more tallies on the numbers of hours he'd spent editing stories, more Michigan State memorabilia . . . and far more energy and devotion to his students than all of us put together.

Third, I worked with Brian McDowell, our journalist, turned PR guy, turned teacher. After first Jerry, then I and finally Neal were gone, Brian was the last left of *my* "Old Boys' Club" and he took over this program and dedicated himself to keeping it afloat in changing times, and for that we are all so grateful.

Finally, I worked with a magical cast of *student* characters who made this place special and animated. These talented and sometimes wacky kids—combined with my three unique colleagues—made every day a new adventure in the J-program.

I treasure my five fabulous years here, my honorary membership in the "Old Boys' Club," my lasting friendships with these wonderful guys, their special spouses and families, and with the hundreds of students and alumni who make the Morrisville J-program the phenomenal family it is . . . and for that I continue to feel very "LUCKY" indeed.

Jon Landman ('94), GM of WCVM, and Mary Ellen Mengucci

47

Lots of Teachable Moments

By Edward J. Conzola

Professor of Journalism Since 2002

One of the things that attracted me to the journalism program at Morrisville State College was its emphasis on hands-on learning. I remember my own entry into the field of journalism and the feeling that I had learned more the first week on the job than I had all through graduate school. So it shouldn't be surprising that I strongly believe that the best way for a student to learn the skills necessary to succeed as a journalist is to do the actual tasks demanded by the profession.

To put that belief into practice, I try to make my classroom assignments as real-life as possible. And nowhere am I more successful at that than in my Sports Writing class.

A requirement of Sports Writing is that each student cover at least one "major" event for a daily newspaper. The events covered have ranged from the state boy's volleyball championships (for the Albany Times Union) to the NJCAA hockey national championship (for the Minot, N.D., Daily News).

But one event stands above all the others in my memory – because of the deadline writing experience it offered.

The students were covering the State University of New York Athletic Conference basketball championships for several newspapers. As it turned out, two of the teams we had been following throughout the tournament met in the men's final, so two students were covering the same event from two very different perspectives.

That in itself offered a great teachable moment, but the real challenge for the students came when the game was played. The contest had been scheduled to start at 8 p.m. Our deadlines (for both papers) were 11 p.m. Plenty of time (we thought) to cover the game, get the requisite post-game interviews and file the stories – even though the tournament site did not have Internet access and we would have to drive to a nearby college to file.

The title game we were covering was preceded by the women's championship game, which started at 6 p.m. Unfortunately for us, that game (which we were also covering) went into overtime, so the start of the men's game was pushed back roughly 40 minutes. Once the game was finally underway, it was a slow affair, with repeated time-outs and fouls that drew it out longer than the expected 60-75 minutes.

The contest finally ended around 10:20, and the students rushed off to get their interviews. It was nearly 10:40 by the time we were in the car on our way to file.

The students found themselves in the back seat, typing furiously on their laptops and hoping their batteries would hold out. We got to the college from which we were filing at about 10:50, did some very quick edits on the stories and pushed the button to send them to our respective papers almost simultaneous with the clock striking 11. We had made deadline, and both papers ran the stories virtually unchanged from what we had sent.

Where else but Morrisville would you get that kind of experience with deadline pressure and the need to adapt to a difficult situation?

Edward "E.J." Conzola joined the faculty in 2002 after a rich career in journalism. Most recently, he taught journalism at Utica College. Before that, he was advisor to The Quill, the student newspaper at Russell Sage College in Troy, NY. He has worked as a reporter for a number of newspapers, including the Daily Gazette In Schenectady, The Albany Times-Union, The Press & Sun Bulletin in Binghamton, and the Adirondack Daily Enterprise. He worked as publicity coordinator for the Saratoga Performing Arts Center, Saratoga Springs, NY. In 1980 he chronicled the Lake Placid Olympics for The Daily Olympic Digest. E.J. has served as chairman of the Morrisville State College Journalism Department since September 2005.

48

"Harvard of Central New York"

By Gladys L. Cleland
Professor of Journalism since 1996

Each day, I tell the students, "You are studying at the Harvard of Central New York." I believe it! Morrisville State College is a vibrant place to learn both academic and life's lessons. Why shouldn't we consider ourselves among the top? We are. As of this writing, I am halfway through my 12-year teaching career in the Journalism Program and at WCVM Media. I never dreamed the students I have encountered along this journey would change my life in the ways they have. These students are bright, articulate, evocative, tolerant, and spiritual. They offer a frame of reference that is beyond their years. Their histories produce scenarios and tales that will stop you in an instant. Some have never experienced positive feedback; others have never experienced failure. Trying to teach both types is a jolt to the senses, a wake-up call to "their" real world, and a warm hug highlighting the complexities of their stories.

Teaching in the Journalism Program has made me a different person: a content provider, an evaluator, a mentor, a friend ... and, most importantly, a "sparent" – a spare parent. I did not seek this role; I know it was not in the original job description but, somehow, at the Harvard of Central New York, I've become one. My department colleagues and I have grappled with the many life altering issues our students bring us, including death. These experiences change you as a teacher and change the way you approach your own life. For me, the students' stories have challenged my views about student development and basic human interaction. One constant I maintain is: "If you believe, you will achieve." I'll always be "'GladBo' – the academic Rambo," but my teachings reflect a greater essence of spiritual groundedness, interspersed with the offerings of journalism ethics, methodology, and technology.

The Journalism students, past and present, have become an extended part of my world - my family - of me. I learn with them, laugh with them, and cry with them. I cry harder when they pass on from this world at a young age. I have to realize, even in death, they continue to write and edit their own stories.

So, at the Harvard of Central New York, I look forward to never growing up and always maintaining my insatiable sense of curiosity, drive, and ambition. Conceptualizing and authoring a bachelor's degree in Videojournalism is an introspective reflection of these qualities and a reminder of who I am and who I have become at Morrisville State College. I hope to infuse these same qualities in our newbie communicators for their next adventures. Most of all, I hope to ignite the students' desire for quality of life and integrity. To teach a journalist is not just about outlining the elements of the story – it's about outlining the elements of one's soul.

Gladys L. Cleland is an associate professor of Journalism, joining the MSC faculty in 1996. She holds a Master of Arts degree in mass communication from the University of Florida and a Master of Science degree in higher education from Syracuse University. She is currently pursuing a doctor of management degree in organizational management and leadership from the University of Phoenix. Cleland's 20+ years of professional experience includes reporting and producing for print, broadcast, and online media; media and public relations; and serving as the premiere faculty intern at the former CNN-SI division in Atlanta. In May 2006, she was awarded a SUNY Chancellor's Award for Excellence in Teaching. Cleland continues to work professionally in the local, regional, and national media.

49

McDowell: "Mover and Shaker"

By Neal Bandlow
Professor of Journalism 1972—1999

It is time to set the record straight. So much has been written and ver-
bally acknowledged about the contributions in the first 40 years of Morrisville's Journalism Program by Jerry "Saddle Shoes" Leone, the program's founder; and yours truly, the hooligan from Michigan. One name,
however, continues to be missing in action when citing the "movers and
shakers" of those four decades: Brian McDowell!

For a moment, let me set aside Brian's loyal 13-year commitment to
our Journalism Program and take a glance at his overall 23-year dedication to Morrisville State College. Mostly unheralded, Brian's tireless and
long-standing service to the entire college is unparalleled. Nobody—I
repeat, *nobody*—among faculty and staff has logged more hours of "work
time" in those two-plus decades of employment on campus.

Arriving on campus in 1985, Brian served 10 exemplary years as the
college's public relations officer, director of alumni activities, and sports
information director, often simultaneously performing all three duties.
Trust me: in my 27 years at Morrisville, I can't name one other person
who while working in those job descriptions on campus was as thoroughly prepared, responsible and dedicated as Brian.

Eventually, he even found time to sneak over to our journalism area
and teach part-time as a news writing lab instructor, beginning around
1990 or so. Lucky for us, it was the beginning of a now ongoing 18-year
"love affair" for Brian and the J-Program! He was a natural in the classroom, and slowly, he began to fit in with the unique "we are family" approach to our program. Then, shortly before Leone's retirement in 1995,
Brian approached "Big Jer" and indicated he would like to apply and
come on-board as a full-time faculty member. The answer was "thumbs
up," and the rest is now history. Brian stepped into our starting lineup.
Little did he know, however, that he would become part of the most diffi-

cult period of our program's 40-year history—the late 1990's and first seven years of this century.

Declining journalism enrollment on our campus and major changes overall in the communications industry slowly changed the focus of this once elite two-year program, from one of continued growth and stability to a premise of "crisis survival."

Enter "mover and shaker" McDowell:

* His guidance was instrumental as Journalism Chairperson from 1996 to 2005, including never losing sight of the program's original mission 40 years ago-focusing on the basics and emphasizing "good journalism is based on good reporting."

* His continued commitment to an electronic update for the J-Program and the newsroom. Case in point: In the fall of 1999, Brian made sure the J-Program was one of the first 16 programs on campus to participate in the college's ThinkPad University initiative, requiring Morrisville students to use laptop computers. He engineered the move from 'copy-and-paste' layout to paginated layout on the computer, and advised the move to the Online CHIMES as well. He continues to advise the editorial side of the CHIMES while also supervising layout for print and online editions.

* He recognized that "change" was inevitable to the survival of the print portion of the J-Program, and in an effort to increase student enrollment he researched and introduced a four-year Bachelor of Science degree in "Journalism and Communication for Online Media." That program was approved in 2007. Brian emphasizes that this program also "builds on the strength of the college's current associate in applied science degree in Journalism Technology." In addition, his program ties in with the college's mission, offering innovative programs leading to associate and baccalaureate degrees in technical education. Brian's enthusiasm and marketing of this degree is infectious, and I'm betting it will be successful.

* His continued support of the J-Program's broadcast area and potential four-year degree in videojournalism, also on the horizon via Professor Gladys Cleland.

* Finally, the focal point of this man is Brian's never-ending, faithful commitment to the emotional needs and welfare of each student in the J-Program. He never quits encouraging students to broaden their horizons and explore new ideas. More importantly, his office door is always open to any student who needs assistance or personal counseling, embodying the "we are family" concept from years past, an aspect of the program that is so precious to me.

Without question, we celebrated the 40th year of journalism at Morrisville in July, 2007, largely due to Brian McDowell's efforts and contributions to keeping the J-Program—as we all know it—alive and functioning during the "lean" years. Thanks, Brian ,for being an indispensable part of a program that has so much meaning to me, the other former J- faculty, and more than 1,500 journalism grads.

Neal Bandlow "holding court" in 1977
- Photo by Nancy Cardillo

SECTION 6

———

How Morrisville Still Influences Today

50

"A World Apart"

By David Jicha
Class of 1981

A few weeks ago I was standing behind a pulpit in my little church paying homage to my pastor. It was pastor appreciation day and I was one of several people called upon to speak.

I began by relating memories of teacher figures that have impacted my life, but noting that at the age of 47 the memories fade. As they do, certain teachers remain a fixture in my life while others fade away. I recalled one or two high school teachers who stirred up vague memories – for various reasons ranging from respect to fascination – but I then directed my little speech toward the teenagers in the small group by telling them, "You know, college is a world apart from high school. When you get to college, you're studying the things you really want to learn about, whereas in high school you study what they make you study. Most of you out there will not remember in 20 years the algebraic formulas they are stuffing into your heads today. But in college it all changes".

Images immediately popped into my head: Jerry Leone's saddle shoes; Neal Bandlow's manic pacing as he drove home points; Joe Quinn's grandfather-like demeanor as he taught with his hands delicately facing each other, fingertip to fingertip; Charlie Hammond casually explaining the "Clamplate Orgy" and his days at radio station "K-UNT" (he misspoke intentionally to see if we were paying attention); and John O'Connor, who I personally considered the "bully" of the five professors who would change my life.

"Why do I remember all of these details", I thought as I prepared my talk. I remember them because the J program at Morrisville was,

116

and by all recent accounts that I see, is blessed with talented and dedicated teachers. Leone's specialty was photography, but make no mistake – he had opinions on everything. And I never saw the man lose his cool. Bandlow absolutely captivated his class of '81 on one of the first days of lecture when he relayed his Vietnam experience of walking point on a patrol when the bullets started flying. He was hit in the shoulder and the tumbler bullet traveled through his torso and exited his back. He remembers waking up with no fingernails because he was trying to dig himself underground while the assault was taking place. Why do I remember that after 28 years when I have trouble remembering what happened yesterday?

I remember the nervousness that I felt but tried so hard not to show "the bully" John O'Connor as I informed him that not only did I want the editor-in-chief position on the school magazine "Arcadian", but also the graphics editor position on the school newspaper "Chimes". And I remember my fear of that man turning into respect when he told me that he respected my hunger for both positions.

And I remember the cold stare I got from Professor Hammond when I turned in my first advertising project - a mock print ad done "character profile" style – depicting him as the subject for a brand of scotch whisky. Ah, memories.

The point is this: certain people come into your life that you will always remember. I have been blessed with a select group that for whatever reason taught in a little cow-town in upstate New York.

When I started my little tribute to the pastor who has played a huge part in my little life, the first thing I thought about was teachers. Jesus Christ was a teacher; my profs at Morrisville were teachers, and my pastor is a teacher. I am so thankful for each and every one.

51

Between 'Hanged' and 'Hung'

By Nancy Cardillo
Class of 1977

I attended MATC for Journalism by sheer luck. I'd applied to three SUNY schools for Secretarial Science, but my high school guidance counselor told me I should utilize my English skills and suggested Journalism and Morrisville. After a trip to see the campus and meet the faculty, I fell in love (for the first time on that campus, but not for the last!).

Now, looking back some 30+ years later, I still believe those years at MATC to be two of the most important years in my life. I did transfer to Utica College but, at best, that merely complemented my time at MATC. I never felt cheated by not having attended a larger school; on the contrary, I believe the small-town atmosphere at MATC, the navigable campus and small classes contributed to a wonderful college experience – no, a wonderful *life* experience.

I am now employed as a freelance writer – a career I'd dreamed about since my first job at an ad agency. I could not have gotten to where I am without Morrisville. Neal Bandlow, Jerry Leone, Joe Quinn and Dan Reeder taught me how to write well and still influence my writing today (I will never forget Dan Reeder's rather visual explanation in editing of the difference between "hanged" and "hung"). Jerry taught me my way around a 35mm camera (which helped pay my way through UC). Charlie Hammond introduced me to the world of advertising.

My roommate, Donna Bliss, and I still remain in contact and, on the rare occasions we see each other, it's as though we've never left campus. I am still in close contact with several other MATC grads – friendships I cherish and hope to keep for a lifetime. I lost one of those dear friends, Gary Izzo, to cancer, but our good times started in high school, continued at MATC and well into our 40s.

I am still in contact with both Neal and Carol and Jerry and Barb, as I know many J-grads are.

We shared more than classes and lab time at MATC. We partied on the weekends at the Towne House and the Fort. We worked side by side at WCVM and the Chimes. We had teachers who were also our friends, and whose doors were open whenever we needed a lift, a laugh or a good swift kick in the butt. Who can forget Neal "holding court" in his office, before dragging us all to the Towne House on a Friday afternoon? Electric typewriters. Jockeying for position at the photo dryer in the darkroom. Jerry's saddle shoes. The blizzard and the heat wave that gave us mention on the Tonight Show all in the same week. Grub Day. The Charlie Daniels Concert. Convocation.

I still can't believe all we crammed in to two short years, and I am amazed at how the education I received at MATC and the people I met there still have a positive impact on my life so many years later.

Nancy is the founder of More Than Words, a marketing and public relations firm based in Amherst, NY. Its slogan? "All the right words in all the write places." She can be reached at nancy@morethanwords.org.

1977   **Today**

52

Forty Years is a Long Time

By Kevin Lake
Class of 1992

Forty years is a long time in American history when you think about what has happened in this world: the fall of the Berlin Wall, the two Iraq wars, the fall of communism, the space program, and the Boston Red Sox winning the World Series. One wonders how so much history can be enveloped in that short amount of time.

If you think about the number of journalism majors who have come to Morrisville, graduated and made their mark on society—then those 40 years of history don't seem that daunting. These Journalism grads don't just live here in New York. They are spread out throughout the country, covering events like they did here on campus with a love for what they do that surpasses all understanding.

While I have not personally had the opportunity to pursue my journalism career, like a lot of other graduates of this program, I have spent a lot of time this year pondering the "where have I been since leaving Morrisville" moments in my life. In 1992, when I graduated from Morrisville, there were a lot of people who said that the journalism program should be one of the first programs offered at the college on a four-year level. I'm glad to see that is finally going to happen.

Little did I know in my senior year, that I would follow the path of a moment inspired during an advertising class with Mary Ellen Mengucci. My assignment was to create an advertising campaign for the Florida Marlins. They were baseball's newest franchise that year and I was assigned the task in class of creating a marketing campaign to attract fans to South Florida games. That fictional campaign would follow me for most of the next 11 years of my life.

In 1996, shortly after getting married to Sarah, my one and only love whom I met on campus in Morrisville, we moved to South Florida and I purchased season tickets for the Marlins. For the next seven years I lived the dream of the baseball fan that I had envisioned in Mengucci's class. I was able to witness—as a fan and journalist—history in the making, when the Florida Marlins became the fastest team from inception in Major League Baseball history to become world champions. There wasn't a moment that went by that year that I didn't think of my journalistic days in Morrisville covering sports for the Chimes and as news editor at WCVM.

One of the first stories that I had published at Morrisville was the Breeder's Cup World Championship horse racing event. To this day, I am still affiliated with this event. This year, the 24th edition of this historic racing day will be held at Monmouth Park in Oceanport, New Jersey, less than an hour from my current home. I have applied to be a part of this program and hope to continue the coverage of this historic event that I started 15 years ago in the small town we have come to love in central New York.

While this reunion has actually been the first time I have visited the campus since my graduation, I am always reminded of the sports conversations I had with Neal Bandlow regarding his beloved Detroit Tigers. I will never forget and will always cherish the moments that I had here on campus—not only for my journalistic days, but also for my courtship with Sarah.

53

We Kept Laughing for Two Years

By Deborah Kaelin McCaffery
Class of 1974

The most significant story I ever covered in my career as a reporter/ editor was when I worked for a small-town weekly newspaper. It was 1978; I had only been out of Morrisville four years. The piece was actually one of the few editorials I ever had the opportunity to write. I would like to think it helped convince the voters to abolish the Union Ticket that had been in existence for years. Every once in a while there is talk about resurrecting it, but fortunately, it hasn't happened.

Morrisville continues to impact me today. I have kept in touch with faculty and classmates over the years. When approached to serve on the alumni board of directors I did so without hesitation, a position I still hold today.

If I had it to do it all over again, I might not have taken the first job offer that came along. I might have waited, or I might have gone on to complete my bachelor's degree. Actually, I think I would have taken the necessary courses to become a research librarian. I knew newspapers had morgues, but I didn't know there were librarians in charge of them. What a treasure! The hunt for a news clip is challenging, and the find oh-so-rewarding.

My fondest journalism memory while a student at Morrisville? This is difficult because there are so many. I often describe my time at Morrisville as two of the best years of my life. No lie. I vividly remember our first class with Jerry Leone. He conducted it like an interview. He instantly created nicknames for everyone. He got to know us very quickly. He made us laugh, and we kept on laughing for two years.

During that first class, Jerry asked us why we chose to attend Morrisville. My answer was because it had the only two-year journalism program in the state. He seemed pleased with that answer. I didn't know at the time that he had started the program.

It was during our 25th reunion in 1999 that I realized how much I missed the hustle and bustle of the newsroom. Our reunion was in October. The following June, I accepted the position of news librarian/clerk at The Daily Star. My new job made me recall the time Neal Bandlow had us write our own obits during a writing class. I thought at the time that it was an odd assignment, one that some students were having fun with but I wouldn't need to know.

How wrong I was. Very recently I had to write an obituary for a 26 year-old who had been killed that morning in a motorcycle accident, with bits and pieces given to me over the phone by his crying, grieving mother. That was a tough assignment, but she thanked me over and over.

The itch to report strikes me every now and then, but my place is tucked away in the back of the newsroom amidst a stack of multi-colored file cabinets filled with files of clips and microfilm!

Deborah Ann Marie Kaelin McCaffery lives in Cooperstown, NY and works at The Daily Star in Oneonta. She previously worked at the Stamford Mirror Record, Cooperstown Freeman's Journal and the New York State Historical Association Research Library.

She's married with one son, and her hobbies include auctions, yard sales, Jumbles and crossword puzzles.

54

I Write For Geeks

By Barbara Strollo Wetmore
Class of 1977

Sometimes I wake up in the middle of the night, bolt upright to a sitting position, and cry out to myself, "I am not a technologist! How did I get here?"

Oh, that's right. I studied and got my degree in journalism from SUNY Morrisville in 1977. I followed a boyfriend from there to Clarkson University, where I got another degree in technical communication. From there, I got hired by IBM to write instruction manuals for software products. And I've been there ever since.

I didn't wind up a journalist. But I did wind up a writer . . . and a bit of a technologist. My most significant piece of work? The *Network Control Program Installation and Resource Definition Guide.* Surely you've heard of it. It's a best seller among systems programmers.

These days I find myself in the world of the Web. Who among us doesn't find ourselves there these days? I'm an editor for a site called IBM developerWorks. I work with authors to publish technical articles about open standards-based technologies for software developers.

I have the good fortune of living in Raleigh, North Carolina, the same place Jerry Leone himself now lives. We get together from time to time, along with other journalism alums who live in the area, including my first roommate, Fran Yeronick; and one of my floormates from Helyar Hall, Diane Kogut. What a great gift to still have these connections!

When I think back to my days in the journalism program at Moo'ville, I realize the greatest gift I received there was the attention and genuine care and guidance I got from the professors. Big Jer, of course; Neal Bandlow; Dan Reeder; Charlie Hammond; Joe Quinn; Lisa Boulanger. I was an O.K. student in high school, but I flourished in college because of the passion these professors had for the program and for their students. I now have a son who is a freshman in college, and I wish for him the same relationships with teachers who care. Thank you—all of you journalism professors from 1975 to 1977—for all you gave to me: the knowledge, the skills, and most of all, the confidence and belief in myself that I could make it in the great big world that lay ahead.

Barbara Strollo Wetmore, Journalism 1977, is a software engineer with IBM in Research Triangle Park, NC. Although she got sucked into the left-brained world of computer science, she has remained dominated by her right-brain for 30 years and has used her communication skills to develop information products for IBM. She is currently an editor for IBM developerWorks (www.ibm.com/developerworks). She lives in Cary, NC with her husband and two children. You can reach Barbara at bwetmore@us.ibm.com.

1977

2007

55

Ink Is In My Blood

By Nicole A. (Quill) Weinstein
Class of 1990

There is no way to even describe the impact Morrisville has had on my career. Neal Bandlow is STILL one of the most respected people I have had the pleasure of knowing. I took everything he had to say to heart and have applied it to all I do. Ink is in my blood; I have never been happier than when I was working at a newspaper, knee-deep in deadline pressures. I still remember, to this day, the first thing Neal said to us in our first Journalism class of 1988: "If you are in this class thinking that you will make money in Journalism, then you are in the wrong career." SO TRUE!

Since I have two small beautiful children, I have had to make money and now look forward to the day when I can return to "real" journalism. Thanks to Morrisville, Neal, Jerry and Charlie for giving me almost 17 years of happiness in my chosen career!

After graduating from Mo'Ville in 1990, Nicole attended SUNY New Paltz, graduating with a BA in Journalism in 1992. She worked at several local papers throughout the years, making brief forays into PR and grant writing. Her last newspaper job was with the Register-Star in Hudson, NY, where she was the daytime Managing Editor, overseeing not only the Reg, but the Daily News, its sister paper in Catskill. She now works as a Senior Public Information Specialist for the NYS Office of Mental Retardation and Developmental Disabilities as one of a two-member department, writing and designing newsletter articles, brochures, etc. She married Paul Weinstein on June 5, 1999, and they have two children: Samuel and Delia.

Neal Bandlow in 1975

56

Research, Review, and Revise

By Thomas Leone

Class of 1985

I remember my first byline. I was in high school, clerking in the sports department at the local daily. Boy, I was thrilled: my name in print! I learned shortly thereafter what I was truly feeling: pride.

My experiences at Morrisville taught me the importance of taking pride in my work. If my name was on it, I made sure it was something I could be proud of.

It was more like a newsroom than a classroom; Dad, Neal, Charlie, and Joe instituted that from Day 1. And our assignments seemed more important than something that we did for a grade. They were our Editors -in-Chief, and they taught us to complete our assignments as if our jobs depended on it. Hmmmm.

We were introduced to writing style and the importance of it. Editing and meeting deadlines. Critical attributes. I chose the technical writing path following Morrisville. Today, when I distribute my IBM information centers for review, you better believe I've researched, reviewed, and revised.

Dad and his staff proved it can be fun to learn. And boy, did we have fun! Whether it was getting the Chimes out or putting together photo portfolios for Dad, those were invaluable experiences.

Thank God for Dad and Neal and Charlie and Joe and Gooch, and for the guy whose idea it was to contact Dad about starting the Journalism program at Morrisville! One of Dad's biggest regrets was not being able to stay more in touch with all of you. He misses you all dearly. I see it in his face and hear it in his voice whenever I call him or see him. Bandlow, too.

My Morrisville was discussing sports with Neal over a couple of beers at the Fort. Late nights in the darkroom. Parties with J-students new and old.

My Morrisville was clerking for the local daily in high school.
My Morrisville was at the dinner table each night as a young boy.
My Morrisville was a family. Jerry's kids! I lived it and I loved it. Full of pride.

In addition to being the son of Barb and Jerry Leone, Tom is a technical writer based in Lighthouse Point, FL.

Jim Johnson, Nancy Cardillo and Frank Eltman at the 40th Reunion.
Publisher's note: Their work in conceiving (Nancy's idea), organizing, and editing this book was a mammoth undertaking—and a selfless act of service to the Journalism Program that stands alone in our 40-year history.
- Photo by Kim Jackson, '78

57

It's Great Being One of "Jerry's Kids"

By Frank Eltman

Class of 1978

It is a scene that is burned in my memory.

One day while working on the sports desk at The Oneida Daily Dispatch in the early 1980s, Jerry Leone appeared as if out of nowhere, standing at the front counter, asking to speak with me.

Jerry and Neal Bandlow were no strangers to the Dispatch, since they both lived in Oneida and numerous alums got their start in journalism at the small Madison County daily: Norm Landis, Mike Sorenson, Mike Gormley, Phyllis Montague-Harris, and Jack Durschlag, to name but a few.

Jerry, of course, was an icon to me. We had never really been close at Morrisville; I think I was a bit intimidated by him, to be honest. He was the legend who started the program, after all. Neal was my faculty adviser, and I was probably closer with Lisa Boulanger since she was the Chimes adviser, where I worked after leaving the ranks of WCVM under a cloud of controversy.

Anyway, Jerry gives me a big hello and asks if we can speak. He needs a favor.

Anything, Jerry. What can I do?

"My son Tom wants to be a journalist. He's still in high school, but I wonder if you have any openings for an assistant, or a clerk?"

As the sports editor at the Dispatch, I WAS the entire department. No assistants, no clerks, and about two dozen high schools to cover, not to mention the odd story on Morrisville, Colgate or even Syracuse University teams.

Somehow, though, I had managed to convince my bosses that I needed some help churning out all this copy, and they agreed to let me hire a clerk at minimum wage, which was probably around $2 an hour back then. (Heck, I was only making $200 a week as sports editor!)

We worked on IBM Selectrics and had to ``scan'' all the copy into what was one of the earliest incarnations of a desktop computer—page by page. All the stories, all the agate. It was labor intensive.

The timing of Jerry's visit could not have been more perfect.

``Sure, Jerry, we have an opening. Tell Tom to come by the office tomorrow at 7 and we'll get him started.''

I am not sure if you can measure the pride I had at that very moment. I wanted to burst.

Jerry Leone, the founder of the Morrisville journalism program, was asking me to show HIS kid the rudiments of the newspaper business. I was honored, awed, and anxious.

Tom came in the next night, and proved to be an asset immediately. Of course, osmosis gave him more newspaper savvy than other 17-year-olds; he couldn't help but pick up some of what his dad was drumming into kids' heads down on Route 20.

Tom was always on time, always had a great attitude, never called in sick to hang with his pals on a Friday night. There was just one problem: H-e ... t-y-p-e-d ... v-e-r-y ... s-l-o-w-l-y. That helped earn him the nickname ``Lightning Leone,'' a sobriquet he wore with great pride. And he eventually got faster on the keyboard, to be fair.

Tom worked with me for a couple of years before he went off to Morrisville and eventually earned his own journalism degree in the program his father started. Later, his brother Chris would also work with me at the Dispatch for a brief time.

Although I have always felt part of the Morrisville journalism family, I especially cherish the close ties with the Leone family. There has been more than one occasion at Morrisville celebrations like the 40th anniversary this summer where, out of the blue, you heard someone yell, ``Lightning!''

It wasn't a warning about the weather; just an old sports editor reuniting with his clerk.

Two of Jerry's kids, back in town.

58

Two Years That Shaped So Many

By Keith Semerod

Class of 1974

Two years that shaped so many individuals... Pre-class meeting with Jerry Leone in Charlton Hall. One of his statements was something along the lines of "Look at the person on either side of you. They probably won't finish this program." Damn! I knew that would be me.

First classes with Neal Bandlow. His first class was our initial Journalism class. Lectures on an overhead projector. Notes hurriedly scribbled. A staged fight in the STUAC Theater.

Charlie Hammond was a man who imprinted real journalism to 18-year-old kids and made it so realistic. This is what I was here for. Charlie was the advisor for WCVM. At that time, his favorite song was Big Brother and the Holding Company's "Down On Me." I still think of him when I hear that song.

The impact that these gentlemen had on me was that they poured their lives into teaching. They taught us that giving all of yourself to the occupation you love pays dividends for years to come. There was a passion that went beyond anything any of us had ever witnessed. They let us into their lives and showed us that learning is something that happens not necessarily only in a classroom. Thirty fine years later, incidents, statements and conversations are still relevant and still ring clear.

Was it the times? Was it the people? This was happening during Watergate -- When music was on vinyl -- When smoke and electricity coursed through our brains and produced a camaraderie and friendships that are still rich and fruitful all these years later.

A short thank-you note to the men who orchestrated the two year experience. Who impacted much more than they may be aware of. They forged our dependency on regular pilgrimages to Morrisville. They forged a chain of green and white that links our hearts and minds to a tiny town with a small school and with a giant impact on so many lives. Good times, good times.

Keith Semerod is a 1974 SUNY Morrisville graduate in Journalism and holds degrees in Marriage and Family Counseling from Penn State University and a Masters in Social Work from Marywood University. He is a Licensed Clinical Social Worker and has worked for 25 years as a psychotherapist. Currently, he is the Deputy Administrator of Mental Health and Mental Retardation Programs in Pennsylvania. He is married with one daughter. "My truest friends are Morrisville Journalism people." He wants to buy your old records.

1973   2007

59

Still Flying High After All These Years

By Kenneth S. Paden

Class of 1978

I was not the typical Morrisville journalism student because, the route I took to Mo'Ville was somewhat unique. I learned of Morrisville's journalism program from a cousin who was a Morrisville J-program student, while I was serving as a journalist in the Air Force. By taking night classes offered by a college near the Air Force base, I had earned the equivalent of one year of college credit by the time I was discharged.

So when I stepped on Morrisville's campus, I was already a second-year student, and about five or six years older than my classmates. In addition, the Air Force journalism experience gave me a huge head-start on my Morrisville classmates. Still, there were many nuggets of knowledge to be mined from the likes of Jerry Leone, Neal Bandlow, and the rest of the journalism staff.

My entire Air Force career had been spent on the staff of an Air Force base weekly newspaper, so when I reached Morrisville I had a good idea of what weekly newspapering was all about. But I still wanted to take Bandlow's class on weekly papers. The class's text book, written by William Kennedy, has been my "bible" for nearly 30 years.

Kennedy's book on the weekly newspaper is a tangible reminder of my year at Morrisville. But its Leone's lecturing on f-stops, and Charlie Hammond's advertising lessons, and Joe Quinn's classes on news writing that make the Morrisville experience so unforgettable.

Journalism has been my life for some 35 years. A scant nine months of those 35 years were spent in classrooms at Morrisville College, but those nine months—and more importantly those instructors—have had a life-long impact on me. It is that mark left on me that will draw me back to the Morrisville campus to say hello, and thank you.

Since shortly after Ken Paden graduated from Morrisville, he has been involved in the weekly newspaper publishing/printing business in the Southern Tier of New York. The first several years he was an employee of Twin Valley Publishers, Inc. Since 1985 he has been an owner of his own company, publisher of a number of weekly newspapers, and the printer of many more.

In fact, years ago the Chimes rolled off the presses that Paden now owns! He is married and has two daughters. The older one is a sophomore in college, and the younger one a sophomore in high school. He has lived in and has had his business headquartered in Sidney, NY since 1980.

Lisa Boulanger in 1977

60

Calling Teachers by Their First Names?

By John Van Etten

Class of 1985

I was 20 years old when I entered the Morrisville Journalism program in 1983.

It was there I met three professors who wanted to be called Jerry, Neal and Charlie. I had never called teachers by their first name. Soon I realized my learning experience would never be the same.

Within a week we were writing news stories, developing film, and broadcasting on the air. 'Wow,' I thought, 'these men really do seem to care.' Neal was always " pumped up," and Jerry " hands-on." Charlie was more subdued, but clearly an "advertising icon".

Neal taught me the inverted pyramid style, journalism ethics, and how to cut and paste. Jerry showed us how to use depth of field, write banners, and the skills to one-putt!!

I am not a paid journalist, photographer or a broadcaster. I do, however implement many techniques I learned, and my sales career moved faster. I now review business plans, send broadcast messages, and know the importance of deadlines. I write every day, have been paid for over 20 years, and have managed all kinds.

I also do part-time work announcing basketball, lacrosse and football games.

At the 40-year reunion I asked the program founder Jerry how I should read the names. He said, " John keep it simple, practice, and most importantly, don't overdo it." You see, the curriculum always stressed the basics.

I transferred credits, so I only needed 3 semesters to graduate. I knew the program was special, but now I realize it was great. In total, I spent roughly 45 weeks at this small school with a team that still stands tall. I know this for a fact, because I met the current regime at Charlton Hall.

I am not overstating my affection, appreciation and gratitude for the program and particularly for Jerry and Neal. I was asked to share my thoughts, and this is the truth and exactly how I feel.

John Van Etten is vice president of sales for Quench USA.

Journalism's Convocation Day

61

You Could Accomplish Anything

By Debbie Morrow Borden
Class of 1982

My fondest "journalism memory" was the day Neal Bandlow offered me the Features Editor position with *The Chimes* newspaper.

He and another *Chimes* editor tracked me down on campus, which in itself really impressed me. At this time in my life, I had big dreams of being a sports reporter and writer, but still didn't have a lot of confidence in myself. I was a feature reporter and an occasional sports reporter with *The Chimes*, and had heard we just lost our feature editor. Never did I think I would be asked to take over. But Neal and Elizabeth were standing in front of me, saying, "we want you to be The Chimes Feature Editor."

I think I was so stunned, I said no at first. But there was Neal, with his magnetic, contagious enthusiasm, convincing me that I could do this job, with all the great reasons why. I think I did a fair job that year. It was difficult at times, but rewarding. From Morrisville, I went on to UAlbany, majoring in Political Science and a minor in Journalism (they didn't have a journalism program then). It was a horrible experience after Morrisville, but I earned an internship in TV.

So I went from an aspiring, yet less-confident writer to a behind-the-scenes lackey in the broadcasting world. Ten years in TV-land passed, and I never felt more miserable in my life. When I revisited my dreams and goals again, one thing definitely stood out: I wanted to make a difference somehow. But how would I do that? By honoring one of the few people who really made not only a difference, but a huge impact in my life: Neal Bandlow.

While working full-time, I went to the College of St. Rose part-time and received my M.S. Ed. in teaching. And I earned three different certifications, too: in English (my true love), Social Studies, and Elementary Education!

I became an English teacher, and one of the first people I wrote to after this achievement was Neal. I had to make sure he knew not only what a difference he made in my life, but what a wonderful influence he was. He was the kind of teacher I wanted to be for my student's someday -positive, caring, enthusiastic, passionate and honest.

He made you feel like you could accomplish anything; which is what great teachers are supposed to do. I'm married with a 6-year-old daughter and have been teaching for 12 years now. I hope our daughter has at least one great teacher in her life like Neal Bandlow!

Debbie Morrow Borden originally hailed from Scotia and now lives in Burnt Hills, NY. She is "a proud graduate" of the Journalism program at Morrisville College.

62

Roots of the Program Run Deep

By Nicole Reome

Class of 1994

The strength of every family tree comes from its roots.

My first impressions of the Journalism Department at SUNY Morrisville showed me that the roots of that program ran much deeper than any other on campus while the branches of that tree are probably the most twisted.

Following in my older brother's footsteps, I opted to join the program with the goal of building a career in photojournalism. Before I stepped foot in my first class, however, I learned what it meant to be a member of the journalism "family."

Walking into Charlton Hall during a visit to the campus, I introduced myself to Neal Bandlow in what I would learn was *The Chimes* lab.

When I told him who I was and who my brother was, Bandlow grabbed my face with both hands and planted a kiss on my cheek to welcome me to the school. With arms waving in the air, he proceeded to explain that he would be watching over me, at my brother's request, to make sure I stayed away from "guys like him" and out of trouble.

I realized then that I was meeting someone who would become more to my classmates and me than just a professor.

Prior to the start of my freshman year, the program celebrated its 25th anniversary. I attended the event with my brother and realized even more what it meant to be a part of this group.

Watching the interactions of those who came before me with the group charged with guiding me toward a future, it was evident that everyone there had a loyalty and a devotion that could not be measured in words.

With no clear division of class lines, I was welcomed and regarded as "one of them." Just by enrolling in the program, I had become a part of a family.

There was a camaraderie that set us apart from the rest of the school. Others had to go to class. We wanted to go to class.

But it wasn't all fun and games. Together, Bandlow, Jerry Leone, Mary Ellen Mengucci and Brian McDowell kicked our asses and taught us the ropes to make sure that they were sending responsible journalists, photographers and advertising professionals into the world.

Mixed in with those lessons, they taught us to enjoy the simple things in life and think fast on our feet. For example, Leone's finer lessons taught me that saddle shoes will always be cool and film canisters were perfect for holding things like loose change or pot. (Should I say that outloud?)

While we had fun, we also worked hard. But because we worked hard, we almost seemed to learn "by accident." When it came down to it, I found that we were well-equipped with the tools we would need to succeed.

When "real news" broke—like the stabbing at Campus Hill Apartments or the student attacks on Halloween—we were ready to respond and got the word out to the masses.

Nicole Reome is bureau chief for Fulton Daily News (an online publication based in Fulton, NY) and a contributing writer for the Oswego County Business Magazine in Oswego, NY. She has worked professionally in the field of journalism for more than a decade. She and her daughter, 10-year-old Bailey, live in Hastings, NY. She can be reached at nreome@twcny.rr.com.

1994

Today

63

The Teachers Are the Real Asset

By Danielle George

Class of 2005

In the limited two years of the journalism program that I knew to exist, I could only account for a few main attributes that have followed me out of Morrisville that I feel the need to thank the founders for.

As a recent graduate from the year 2005, I've only been living in the "lions' den" of the real world for two years, and certain words of my professors still stick firm in my mind. Granted, I have shifted gears and attended two years at another school in order to get a bachelor's in another program, but that was not without an effort being made to find work with the skills I was given previously.

All the teachers warned us that the real world would be harder, and that they made it easy for us to learn. This is all true, and their honesty and protection from "a cruel reality" should never be taken for granted. It was the hands-on teaching that made such a difference in the real world, and that is why we were so prepared for it.

In my personal experience, comparing what I learned at Morrisville from what I learned at the succeeding college I attended was obvious. I had many more tangible materials to show from my time at Morrisville than from my work at the school that followed.

Taking this knowledge into the field, I've been able to expand and impress more people than I thought possible, as well as impressing myself with what I've done.

All sentiment aside, the teachers were—and are—the real asset to the program, and I hope that never changes. My only concern about the future of the program is that it won't be able to accommodate more students the way it has in the past. I also would have liked to be closer to those with saddle-shoes who began this venture. It only piques my curiosity as to what kind of people they were to have created such a helpful, dynamic tool for the youth who needed it most.

As far as I can tell from the time that I have spent away from the program, but still in close contact with its faculty, there are a few things that have not changed. One constant remains the dedication to the students, and the continuing effort by the faculty to support their previous students, regardless of whether they actually completed the program or not. It really does make us more like a family than anything else.

Another thing that I noticed while working as an editor for *The CHIMES* that rings true to all aspects of the program, are the deadlines. It's a comfort for me to know that our alumni still have the ability to work better under pressure to reach deadlines as they did while in school.

This "In Our Own Words" submission is a perfect example of the need to set, and then extend, the deadlines in order to get the type of participation from alumni needed to complete the project. We used to harass our writers in much the same way. It is a comfort, and a joy to know that some things never change. I will never forget those things throughout my work experience, and through my fond memories of the Journalism Department at Morrisville State College.

Danielle earned a BA at Ithaca College this year. She joined the Ithaca College Circus Club and has performed with other professional circus groups as the Bindlestiff Cirkus, and the Cornell Juggling team. Brian McDowell helped her publish a coloring book—containing her artwork—for a small company in Biscayne Bay, Florida.

Learn more about Danielle at the following URLs:
http://www.daniellegeorge.net
http://www.bubblegumjunkie.com

64

"I Am So Proud of You"

By Sharon A. Driscoll

Class of 1985

The guy in the saddle shoes and the cheerleader would smile and say, "I knew she could do it!" But at times, they did wonder: the spelling was awful, my sentence structure stunk, and they were sure I had never taken English 101 – Small Engine Repair, maybe, but not English 101."

That was back in 1983. I was 20 years out of high school, divorced with three children: aged nineteen, eight and seven. I was in desperate need of an education and someone—anyone—to believe I was capable of more than changing diapers and doing housework.

During my two years in the J program there were times when Professor Neal Bandlow was ready to tear out the few hairs remaining on top of his disguised, but balding head. His faith in my abilities was nothing short of miraculous. He pushed, encouraged and praised. His constant support and guidance helped to boost my self confidence from near zero to, "Not too shabby, Driscoll!"

Jerry Leone, although sometimes aloof and seemingly uninterested in anything except his photography students, of which I was one, cared deeply for the well being of all his students. On graduation day 1985 he stood at the end of the walkway with his arms outstretched and tears streaming down his face as I walked proudly towards him with diploma in hand. If I live to be 100, I will never forget that moment when he embraced me and said, "I am so proud of you. You will just never know!"

An Associates Degree from SUNY Morrisville provided a means to an end; the knowledge necessary to achieve a higher paying position and the ability to feel secure and self confident in whatever path I chose. Although there were a couple of times when Jerry and Neal had to reach out and give me a kick! Like the time they basically pushed me kicking and screaming into an interview with Mike Milmoe, owner of the Bee Journal in Canastota.

Jerry told me that if I could not afford to go on to get my bachelor's degree, the best thing for me to do was go to work for a weekly. *He was right.*

I have not worked for the New York Times, but my career as a journalist has been fulfilling. I have interviewed and photographed prominent political figures and business leaders throughout New York State. A news release I wrote about the first murder in the history of Cazenovia in 1992 was read out loud by Congressman George Wortley to his fellow associates on the floor of the House of Representatives in Washington, DC.

All that I have accomplished since graduating in 1985 would not have been possible without the support and understanding I found at SUNY Morrisville. "Thank you Jerry and Neal for providing me the tools necessary to make and sustain a life for myself and my children."

The college experience had a lasting affect on my family, showing them the importance of a higher education.

"And, that is how I got here."

Since 1992 Sharon has been employed by Madison County as the Public Information Officer/Recycling Coordinator. She previously worked for Rivette and Driscoll Records Management, the Cazenovia Republican, and the Canastota Bee Journal. She has three sons, three grandchildren, and three cats.

Sharon Driscoll in 1985

Sharon Driscoll today

65

A "Heady" Time to be a Journalist

By Tim Arena

Class of 1975

In the fall of 1973, I was among 150 or so incoming Journalism students attending my first class in a lower-level classroom in the new Library building (a space now occupied by the campus store). Jerry Leone, Neal Bandlow, Dan Reeder, Charlie Hammond and Art Pastore were at the front of the room, introducing themselves and describing the upcoming school year. Jerry made it an interactive event by asking all of us to say what made us want to study journalism.

Neal was especially memorable because of his immediate and infectious enthusiasm for journalism as a community service and force of social change. At the time, Neal seemed somewhat radical, with his long blond hair and skepticism about the government and the continuing war in Vietnam (which didn't end until mid-1975). At the same time, he seemed traditional by stressing the importance of concise writing and editing.

During those initial classes, Neal emphasized that it was a vibrant time to be a journalist. He spoke about the efforts of Bob Woodward and Carl Bernstein, reporters for The Washington Post who were writing every day about then President Richard Nixon and the emerging Watergate scandal.

Neal pointed out that Woodward and Bernstein were becoming heroes to many by investigating and reporting on the Nixon administration and enforcing the power of the press. It felt both inspiring and challenging to recognize that journalists—regular people who wrote for newspapers—could be heroic by exposing crimes and corruption.

In 1973 the journalism classroom had an Associated Press teletype machine, printing out news on white rolled paper. In October, after Vice President Spiro Agnew resigned in a political scandal, several journalism students rushed to the teletype machine to read that breaking news story

146

and save the printout as a sort of historic record. Months later, in the summer of 1974, between my freshman and 'senior' years at Morrisville, Nixon resigned as president—largely due to the efforts of journalists.

My fond memories of journalism at Morrisville go beyond national politics. In my two years, *The Chimes* reported on topics including a controversy over creating co-ed dorms (instead of single-sex dorms), a major fire in Helyar Hall, and the effects of an Arab oil embargo (which created long lines at gas stations in Morrisville and nationwide).

During my senior year, it seemed like many of my fellow "J students" flourished at the *Chimes* by writing and editing new editions every week. While students created the stories, photos and headlines, a small printing company in Canastota set the type, headlines and page layouts. That company had a policy not to print or even typeset any kind of profanity. In one issue, a reporter reviewing a concert described it as being part of a "bad-ass weekend." The printed story used the term "bad-xxx weekend."

Working on *The Chimes* related closely to the Journalism program by emphasizing the importance of having well-rounded knowledge of current events, combined with basic writing, editing and photography skills. It was also memorable because it merged the sometimes stressful work of writing and editing news with the simple pleasure of spending time with other students who were equally dedicated to becoming journalists.

Timothy Arena graduated from Morrisville in 1975 and received a BA degree in Communications from SUNY Oswego in 1977. He currently works as an administrator at The New York Times in New York City.

66

The Three "R's" Still Apply

By Jim Coulthart

Class of 1975

The Journalism Technology program at Morrisville is where I learned to write and to effectively communicate. It is fair enough to say the "J" faculty instilled the Three R's in me: Readiness, Realism, and Relevance.

Even though I never pursued a career in print or broadcast journalism, the skills and techniques learned in class, lectures, and in writing labs from Neal Bandlow, Jerry Leone, and Charlie Hammond are utilized *every day* in my correspondence and other business dealings.

These points will no doubt seem familiar to journalism majors from 1967 on to present day:

Readiness: The thoughts expressed when I write are prioritized, organized , and composed in my head. These thoughts *then* go directly to the page by typewriter or word processor…..no hand-written drafts for me. This technique came from numerous story exercises in the writing labs.

Realism: Unless opinion is requested, it's *who, what, when, where, how,* and *why*. Strip away the superfluous words. Stick to the facts. In other words, "omit needless words." The stuff of style books!

Relevance: Knowing how to distill and rank order the essence of a story serves me well. That ability has its roots in all those writing lab exercises. It's amazing how much can be covered in a radio newscast.

When I went on to obtain my four -ear communications studies degree in large lecture halls, journalism theory was more highly prized than the 'hands-on' pragmatic skills taught at Morrisville—until something actually had be accomplished and words placed on the written page.

The 'get-it-done' Morrisville style continues to separate me now from my business colleagues.

In prioritizing news items and scripting all those three minute radio newscasts for WCVM, I developed appreciation for the importance of timing so I know when to wrap things up! My heartfelt thanks go out to Neal, Jerry, and Charlie for teaching me the 3 R's. Likewise, I'm pleased to know these basics are still stressed by today's journalism faculty.

Jim Coulthart is currently a membership representative with the Medical Society of the State of New York. After graduating from SUNY Oswego with a BA in Communication Studies-Broadcasting, he pursued professional careers in marketing, sales, and non-profit agency administration. He also enjoys being an adjunct instructor in sales/marketing for local area colleges.

Coulthart and his wife, Colleen, reside in Oneida, NY. They have two grown children: Sara (Mo'ville Journalism graduate 2000), and Stephen, who is pursuing advanced graduate degrees in international diplomacy.

67

The Dreaded Red Pen

By Deanna Schulmerich

Class of 1991

The two years I spent at Morrisville are some of the best times of my life. I had the typical college experience: parties, late nights, early mornings and much more I cannot tell here. I learned so much—academically and personally—that I credit those two years in shaping me into the person I am today.

Personally, I learned to be tough and to take criticism. Academically, I was taught how to take all the thoughts that were in my head and put them on paper in a clear and cohesive manner that was understandable and informative. I admit now that when I got to Morrisville in the fall of 1989, my writing was bad. For all the dreams I had of being this great writer and thinking I just needed to go to school to polish my skills, I quickly learned that was not the case and I needed a lot of work to even think about getting published. I would just write and hope the reader would be able to follow the thought process I had in my head.

Neal, Jerry and Brian helped me see what my mistakes were and where I could improve and tighten my writing to make it clear and concise, while getting it to flow as a story should. I quickly learned the phrase 'too wordy' from Neal and knew that when I handed in the next assignment, I better have taken the lessons previously learned and applied them to the current assignment or I would again see the words 'too wordy' in red pen on the paper. As much as I hated to see those words in red when I got too long-winded, it was those same red pen marks that gave me praise when I had done something right.

I learned that just because someone criticizes you it does not mean they don't care; it means they see where things can be improved. To this day, I work to make sure that whatever I write is clear and concise and not too wordy. I still have some of those stories I wrote while at Morrisville, both published and unpublished, to remind me of what not to do, and when I feel that something I have written is bad, I look back and see what bad writing *really* is.

Now, I spend much of my time blogging about sports, mainly NASCAR with a little football thrown in once in a while. In each of those entries I try to get the point across without losing the reader, knowing I only have their attention for a few short paragraphs. When I get feedback—good or bad—I take it and apply anything I can to make the next entry better.

Although I only had the pleasure of being at Morrisville for two years, they are ones I always look back on with pride and happiness-and am forever grateful for the lessons I was able to take away from there.

Deanna is currently working in the Rochester Institute of Technology Housing Operations Office. She spends her free time watching and blogging on NASCAR and football, enjoying time with family and friends, and still working toward finding that career-defining job.

68

Balancing New-Age Journalism

By Susana Schwartz

Class of 1991

As a journalist, I am a "mirror" of society. I have to reflect an image of the current and evolving state of humankind. To cast an accurate picture, I have to put aside biases and opinions so as to filter information through a neutral prism. "Allow the reader to decide," as Mo'ville taught me.

That has been increasingly challenging as my two worlds collide: that of my belief in the Constitution, and that of burgeoning technologies I cover that help to mitigate its purpose.

Ironic, since I used to dream of a life akin to that of Woodward and Bernstein, breaking stories like "Watergate" and feeding a public the information they coveted to keep a check on the government.

Somehow, technology rather than politics became the bulwark of society, as most conversation and debate now revolve around social and business networks, devices and gadgets. To make a living as a writer, I have had to exist and even fuel the digital era, but I've had to constantly balance my personal belief—that technology distracts people from life, as opposed to bringing them into it—with the interests of my readers.

One of my biggest internal battles as a person and as a writer came with the ongoing story of government eavesdropping and wiretapping. Key to that ability is complicity by the broadband providers and Internet companies—my audience. Eavesdropping on a phone call is as easy as finding the copper wires that run into every person's home, but with fiber build outs and data, the government is finding it more difficult to spy on average denizens. The encryption technologies and infrastructure for DSL and VoIP services had become obstacles to the government's ability to execute spying programs.

In 1994, the government passed CALEA, which requires broadband and telecom providers to "ensure" that their networks are technologically "capable" of being accessed by authorized law enforcement. In a post 9/11 era, I've had to inform companies of what they need to do technologically and culturally to conform to CALEA. That has been difficult, for in the background, I am cognizant of my lessons in Mo'ville's journalism classes—that abuses of power can be caught only by individuals, whose only means to disseminate that information is through the media. That filtering of personal information had become more arduous in an age where the subjects of criticism are often in bed with those who own the channels.

Working for a right-wing, conservative, there was no room for hypothesizing about CALEA's impact on individual freedoms, for it would be misconstrued as "conspiracy theory." As I had heard more and more shocking information about violations of privacy, I turned to the Internet, which gave me the option to write in an anonymous manner. While the government will focus on the downside of anonymity, I tend to look at the positives as more important to Democracy.

My heart sang with joy when Bandlow's "Gray Lady" sang, as the New York Times broke the news that the NSA was spying on millions of Americans—most of them on watchdog lists for being activists rather than "terrorists" (whatever a terrorist may be). ABC and CNN were the first to show outrage that reporters were allegedly being tracked by the NSA, and individual citizens were outraged that their "trusted" providers gave up their personal data without any warrants or requests for permission.

Verizon, AT&T and others are now in the midst of lawsuits brought by lawyers representing the denizens of the United States, and Congress is debating whether or not it should extend the powers of the government to eavesdrop as technology makes it more difficult, yet at the same time, more simple to spy.

Although I lose a lot of sleep when I think of how to write about Constitutional issues to an audience of technology juggernauts, I am excited to be part of this very volatile time. Technology and Constitutional freedoms have to co-exist, and to be a part of both worlds as a journalist is a unique experience.

I can only hope that Susana "the Technology Writer" can co-exist with Susana "the Individual." The ability to find harmony will depend on the existence of independent media willing to print what corporate-sponsored media increasingly will shun: real information. Infotainment is the new paradigm, and that is why my newest battle has to be "Net Neutrality." Through interviews with powerful people like Google's Vint Cerf, "the Father of the Internet," and FCC Chairman Kevin Martin, as well as the heads of telecom, cable and Internet companies, I will try to fill Cyber "white space" with information that will galvanize people to read the Constitution and play a role in securing the Internet as the last frontier of independent media. The government wants control of it, but I have faith that we will cycle from infotainment to real, hard news again. It will be up to Mo'ville's future journalism grads to ensure that cycle back to truth.

Susana is Editor-in-Chief of Webpreneur Magazine in New York.

69

The '5Ws & an H' benefit Campus Cop

By Perry M. Gordon

Class of 1977

Thirty years have passed since I graduated from the Journalism Technology program at what was then SUNY-Morrisville, or Morrisville Agricultural and Technical College—MATC for short. All things change with time, and we are now Morrisville State College, with a four-year journalism program all but official, unless I've missed the latest news release that made it so.

And perhaps 31 or 32 years have passed since I was first asked by family, friends, and about-to-graduate classmates, "What will you do with a two-year degree in journalism?" I didn't have an answer then. Thirty years later, having turned 50 this past January, the question now becomes, "What have I done with a two-year degree in journalism?" It's an easier question to answer.

After discovering quickly that I was not going to work for *The New York Times*, *The Boston Globe,* or the *Albany Times-Union*, I continued in college, earning a bachelor's degree in political science, a master's degree in English, and nearly a doctorate in English, all interspersed within a longer career in higher education and law enforcement.

Yes, you read that right: I became a campus administrator and a cop, concurrently for the last 13 years, two of the very types that aspiring journalists seek out for the inside story—or for the stonewalled details. But I'm happy to report that, ongoing criminal investigations aside, I'm not the stonewalling type. In fact, I often wince when I'm interviewed by an under-prepared student journalist who arrives at my office without questions and often without a recorder or a note pad, and occasionally I find myself prompting him in the hope that he or she will catch on and ask me a follow-up question that digs deeper.

I sometimes think to myself that Dan Reeder or Neal Bandlow or Jerry Leone or Charlie Hammond or Joe Quinn—would have taught him better than this. For a moment I feel sorry for him that he has never met these men, and I try not to write the story for him, but sometimes the temptation is overpowering. As you might guess, I review the story when it appears in the campus or local paper—and you can be sure that in the next 5 minutes I'm at the keyboard writing clarifications if I think they got the story (or a small detail) wrong. The bureaucrat in me hates to be misquoted, but more than that, the journalist in me hates to see another writer get the facts wrong.

That nose for news—and getting it right the first time—is something I learned at Morrisville under the tutelage of Jerry, Neal, Charlie, Joe, and Dan (these guys don't need last names, having reached iconic status with us), and I try to encourage my students in first-year composition, as well as American literature survey courses, to ask (and answer) the basic questions of Who, What, When, Where, Why and How as they write a narrative reflection, analyze an event, or study an idea in literature.

Start with the basics, I remind them, and the details will fall into place. I also remind them that some of the biggest names in American literature—Mark Twain, Ernest Hemingway, William Dean Howells, and Walt Whitman started as journalists and newspaper reporters. Whether any of my students will become another of those big names, a teacher always has hope.

Does Morrisville still 'impact' me today? My traffic citation reports, accident investigations, crime reports, as well as my memoranda outlining an upcoming campus event, public notice of a bus route change, or a news release on a policy change still adhere to the 5Ws and an H that I learned 30 years ago.

If I have any doubt about how to write a long report, how to convince a judge of the sureness of an arrest, or how to inform the campus of the necessity and reasonableness of a policy change, I remind myself of what I learned 30 years ago on a smaller campus from people whose shoes (saddle or otherwise) I haven't yet filled.

Perry Gordon is now the Assistant Director of Parking & Transportation Services (in charge of the people who write parking tickets, and also making sure the buses run on time) in Oxford, Ohio. He is also a Visiting Instructor (College-Speak for 'part-time faculty') in the English Department at Miami University, Oxford, Ohio. He married (finally!) in 2004 and is the proud "father" of several abandoned domestic rabbits who were rescued in Hueston Woods, near the college campus.

70

Writing My Own Obituary

By Dianne Kogut

Class of 1976

Thirty-three years ago this month, I was given the assignment of writing my own obituary in News Writing 101 by Neal Bandlow. In a freshman class of over 75 students, I pondered the assignment and how I could possibly stand out in a class of wanna-be journalists. It was the investigative times of Woodward and Bernstein that had further inspired me to be at Morrisville, and I had already spent a few of my high-school years pursuing an education and career in journalism. But now, only a week into my fledging journalistic endeavors, I had to write my own obituary.

I thought Mr. Bandlow was crazy. With all the hot topics of the day, I didn't see this as the assignment of a lifetime, but I chose to complete it with the creativity and enthusiasm that had always been my inspiration. So I began with the following lead: Dianne Kogut, 18, was found bored to death in an introductory news-writing class led by instructor Neal Bandlow.

Well, it definitely caught Neal's attention. I had succeeded at writing an obituary with flair and creativity. So began my career as a creative writer and a reporter of feature stories for several publications.

Over the last thirty years, I have doggedly pursued and kept true to my writing. It has been the one thing that has kept me grounded and in touch. And it was those humble beginnings in Morrisville that got me on the right road. The program allowed one to experience all disciplines of the Journalistic world and opened my eyes beyond the written word. I worked at the radio station WCVM and later went on to be a top disc-jockey in a metropolitan establishment thru the disco era and beyond. I became enthralled in photography class by Jerry Leone and discovered a new world thru a view-finder. I later went on to be a local free-lance photographer, and even had the once-in-a-lifetime experience of being an add-on photographer for the National Olympic Committee covering the Junior Olympics in Syracuse.

I have to give credit for a wonderful career to those who truly inspired me. My thanks and gratitude go out to Neal Bandlow for his insight, skill and dedication in inspiring a bunch of twisted individuals in a town with more local bars than locals and more temptations than should be allowed. And a very special thank you to Jerry Leone for creating such a wonderful program, for urging me to continue my photography and for being such a wonderful mentor and friend to this day.

It's been a long, strange trip for sure, and I count myself blessed and fortunate to have been a part of something magical, life changing and even a little weird at times (it was the seventies, after all). I am currently a communications professional and know that it was that strange news writing class back in 1974 that helped get me here.

Dianne earned a BS in Public Relations from Syracuse University in 1979. She spent nine years working for the City of Syracuse, including the Mayor's office (Lee Alexander) for three years.

She's held numerous Marketing and PR positions, most recently for engineering firms in both Syracuse, NY and Raleigh, NC. The last seven years Dianne has been in the Marketing Group of Siemens Medical Solutions / National Service Organization and currently serves as the Manager of Employee Communications, serving over 2,200 employees nationwide.

Dianne Kogut today

157

71

Every Year's a Souvenir

By Nikky (Puderbaugh) Boyle

Class of 1993

In many ways, my current profession had its beginning at Morrisville.

I have my own scrapbooking business. In that capacity, I labor to convince my clients of the need to tell their stories. Not the stories they read in the newspaper, or the ones they see on TV, but the stories of how their parents met, and how they got their nicknames. It's the seemingly mundane details of life that we are rapidly excluding from our memories.

I think scrapbooking ties into my days at Morrisville, because there I learned to use what I know. I am skilled at storytelling and can share that with others through my business. Neal Bandlow drew my attention to my storytelling abilities with his comments on an article I wrote for his class. He couldn't believe that I would go to the trouble to find out which music my subject listened to in the car. Those details have always fascinated me; I go looking for them.

Being managing editor of *The Chimes* helped me appreciate what is important to the layout of a page, too. Jerry Leone taught me to get the pictures to back up the story. Mary Ellen Mengucci taught me how to have fun with it; I love to use humor in my writing. There's a page in my scrapbook of my oldest as a toddler spitting through a toilet paper tube; you can already see the humor. I got awesome pictures (Jerry, you could even see the spittle flying out the end!). I didn't want to destroy what was already perfectly funny, so I wrote next to the pictures about Caitlin razzing the snack food critics for not endorsing her favorites.

As a journalist, the object is to tell the world about the accomplishments of the professional athletes, the atrocities of war, the tragedies that occur in our towns, and all about politics. A journalist brings the world to the home. In scrapbooking, I help my clients tell of the ways they are celebrities. They relate how their families are affected by their loved ones being deployed to Iraq, and how they have overcome the tragedies in their lives. They share their beliefs with their families. As a scrapbook consultant, I help to showcase my clients' stories for the world!

After graduating from Morrisville, Nikky went on to Mansfield U. to get a degree in public relations. Before completing her degree, she married Don Boyle, and they moved to Orlando, FL in 1994. They have two daughters, Caitlin and Kendra, who consume most of Nikky's time. She enjoys volunteering at the girls' school and at her church. She also serves as a substitute teacher.

72

How Did I Get Here?

By Randy Weiss

Class of 1974

Let's zip to the highlights...

Writing encouragement came early for me. Mostly by math and science teachers. Mo'ville surfaced on my radar in 1972 thanks to my hoops coach who toured the campus with his daughter.

"They have journalism. You could play soccer and basketball. Think about it," coach said.

I did. Thirty seconds later, I was hooked. I soon survived Mo'ville's stringent entrance requirements. *Thanks Frank Potter and Larry Baker, wherever you are.* I landed in rookie professor Neal's very first class. Life was a-changin' PDQ!

Neal and the Legend (Big Jer) pushed in new directions. I tried my best and made *The Dean's List*. No, the other one. Heck, brewskis were only 25 cents. Remember? Sure miss those days...

I had early visions of playing soccer for All-World Coach Art Lemery, but it wasn't to be. I sucked in hoops too, but Coach Whitecavage carried me anyway. I sat next to him every game. For both seasons. I graduated in 1974 with great memories and a lifetime of friendships from a fun J-Drill Instructor and another Class Act (Saddle shoes included).

Then I was off to Albany's Siena College. Catholic school after Mo'ville? Tough transition (hello?), but it made Mom and Dad happy. I majored in English. Then Psych. My "touchdown" upon graduation was *Corporate America* -- home on "Lonk Giland" -- Grumman Aerospace in the personnel field. *Writing dreams fading fast...*

Three years later (1979 if you're scoring at home) - I'm married, living in Santa Barbara and working Industrial Relations for an international, mega-conglomerate. Twenty-one stress-laden work years later (2000) – I experience a near-mid-life career crash. *Writing dreams all but dead.* Luckily, a lifeline from a dot.com gazillionaire amigo sparked new creative energies.

As Executive Director of his philanthropic research center (*psssst:* it was only me) – I delved deep into environmental issues and their passionate champions. I crafted and drafted successes for various publications. A veritable writing Mecca!

Then, *The Moment* exploded after a chance meeting far from home as another soccer dad and his autistic son touched my life. Wrote it up! When *Bakersfield Buddies* found daylight during National Autism Awareness Month – there was no turning back.

Free Op-Eds, essays and features were lofted from everywhere, cultivating more paid side-gigs *a la* ghostwriting speeches and editorials, business websites and a humor column for a new women's' mag. Primo back page real estate here secured my *#1 Rear End* stature. Literally. Figuratively.

Fast-forward to now. Got the best job in the world – short of *NY Times Best-Selling Writer.* I'm doing Community Relations for a 50-branch bank along California's Central Coast, including bi-weekly production of a potential Pulitzer Prize Award-winning electronic *Network News.*

"THIS IS eNN!!" as we say.

My *WeissCrax* column anchors Page One. It's not the *NY Daily News Sports* column I envisioned as a Bayport Kid, but that's okay. I'm finally livin' my *All-American Writing Dream,* nurtured 35 years ago at a special -place in rural New Yawk. That's always the Mo'ville in me.

And I'm just takin' off…

-- Thanks for everything, Neal and Big Jer - "Love ya, Dudes!!"

Randy is married, with two wonderful daughters. With 100+ publications & 3 manuscripts in draft, writing is his "drug of choice." He savors family world travel, California living, and jogging Santa Barbara beaches with his dedicated assistant (in picture at right), Cooper.

161

73

Community

By Eric Lodor
Class of 1986

I grew up across the street from the Morrisville campus, at 25 South Street. In August 1984 I crossed the street to attend my first classes with Bandlow, Leone and Hammond. At that time, I was one of the few "townies" to ever go through the program.

Being a townie at Morrisville came with a unique set of baggage. It was hard to convince some people, particularly Long Islanders and other Metro NYC students that their pre-conceived notions of townies were based on myths, urban legends and the occasional bad experience with a local landlord.

Many Morrisville residents had their own set of prejudices and bias. Some had a low regard for the students who invaded our little village every fall, disturbing the tranquility that reigned in June and July.

Town gown relations are always sticky in small, rural college towns. For us townies the college was both a blessing and a curse. A blessing in the jobs it generated for our little town, a curse in the occasional conflicts between students and residents.

As a student, it was difficult to walk this fine line between one community and another. But I wouldn't trade the experience for anything.

I have never really experienced community in any way that could compare to the Journalism Program. Charlie, Neal and Jerry (and now Brian) instilled a tremendous sense of purpose and pride.

I clearly remember that other students regarded Journalism majors as something of a strange cult – particularly those of us who worked until all hours of the night and all day Saturday to publish the Chimes.

They were envious of our close relationships to our professors. Amazed that we could go out and drink a few beers with them. And puzzled that that they actually tried to get to know us as people.

Clearly, there was an energy about the whole endeavor that was, for many of us, intoxicating. I would venture that very few of us have been fortunate to have experienced that same sense of community in our subsequent higher education or our careers. It was a very special time and a very special place with the best teachers we could have ever hoped for.

However, the energy that seemed to define the program, and to a lesser extent the college and town, has ebbed over the years. Sadly, the college and village today seem to exist in two separate dimensions.

Like many small towns in Upstate New York, the village has fallen on hard economic times. Many of the small businesses that once relied on students and faculty patrons have withered or disappeared entirely.

Many of the current faculty are part-time instructors who have no connection to the community. And, it seems that the full-time faculty seldom set down roots in the town anymore.

Change is inevitable. The demographics of the student population have changed. The mission of the college itself has had to change along with it. I'm confident that with Brian at the helm, Journalism at Morrisville can bridge the past and the future to transform into an outstanding 21st century program.

I hope that both the college and village communities can recapture their once vital energy. The college, the town, the state and even the world will be a better place for it.

Eric Lodor received a BA in Rhetoric from Harpur College and a MS in Technical Communication from Miami University. He is Senior Manager for Intranet Applications with the Kroger Company in Cincinnati, OH. He resides in Loveland, OH with his wife MaryLynn ('88) and three children: Cameron, Austin and Michaela.

74

Morrisville Memories

By Carla DiMenna Thompson
Class of 1974

It was a long time ago, but it is still easy for me to remember Morrisville. Oregon is beautiful, and I love it here, but when I close my eyes I can still see the old houses with slate roofs, the historical markers, the winding roads, and the old bridges. I remember the bike rides and car trips in upstate New York, and sometimes when my mind wanders --I think about Morrisville and those pretty little towns in upstate New York.

When I think of Morrisville I always give thanks for the many good things that I experienced there. I am so grateful for the time I spent there. It was only two years of my life. Just a few months! How could it possibly have been so important?

Morrisville changed my life.

I remember sitting in front of a manual typewriter (no laptop, no desktop, not even an ELECTRIC typewriter!) Just a big metal typewriter and I was expected to pour out what I was thinking. I remember being told to make the words appear on the page. Sometimes it was just "typing,." but sometimes, it was much more. I know I learned to think, and express what I was thinking, while sitting in that classroom in front of those typewriters.

I have vivid memories of j-students taking pictures of each other with Pentax cameras. I remember struggling to wind lengths of film around metal spools in the darkroom. I remember cutting and pasting (literally, not on a computer) stories for the newspaper.

Most of all, I remember the people I met during that short time: Mr. Leone, Mr. Bandlow, Mr. Hammond, Mr. Reeder, Mr. Jackson, Mr. Goetcheus of the drama department, Mrs. Helmer (I never called them by their first names!!) and the many friends from the famous Journalism Class of '74. We had some crazy nicknames for each other. I don't remember them all, but I am sure someone else will. I fondly remember you all!

In the years that came after Morrisville I have accomplished some important things. I have co-authored several text books, I have written articles for journals, magazines and newspapers. I have argued hundreds of cases in the Oregon Courts. I've taught community college, law school and police academy classes. I even debated a local conservative talk show host on the radio! (Everyone said I won the argument, but since it was his show his last words to me were "Well, could be you've got a point there," and then he went to a commercial and our segment was over.) Would I have done any of this if I had not gone to Morrisville? Who knows. I just know it was a wonderful place to begin my adventure.

I send you all my appreciation and affection--- and I promise to keep Morrisville in my prayers, and in my heart, forever.

75

(Our Pulitzer Prize Winner)
The Ultimate Prize

By Jack Durschlag
Class of 1986

It's hard working in the newspaper business day in, day out; I won't lie. Every day we create a new product and hope it's being read, being discussed and most of all, not used to line a bird cage or to train your family dog.

Feedback is essential--both from our peers and our readers. When we're wrong, we get vilified.   So, when we do something wonderful, it's nice to be recognized.

I work for The (Newark, N.J.) Star-Ledger. The Pulitzer was our first, and I was lucky enough to have a small part in it.

On the day of the story, we had been hearing rumors (former) Gov. James E. McGreevey would hold a news conference to discuss a matter of great importance to the state.

I start my work day at 2:30. Rumors said McGreevey would be resigning later in the day--no reason given.

My immediate boss pulled me aside and told me the paper size "might" be changing astronomically. This meant re-booking the paper, changing pages, moving ads and adding pages.

Sure enough, at 4 p.m. that day, the governor told the world he is gay, had an adulterous affair and he's resigning.

Here we were, half of our metro desk on vacation, including two of the editors who run politics and government assignments, and the first edition copy deadline 4 and a half hours away.

By 8:30 p.m., our 10-page comprehensive report included a mainbar, including exclusive details about the affair; sidebars analyzing the political impact, profiling the governor's lover and introducing his successor; and a 70-inch political obituary of the governor's career--all written from scratch.

OK, so how did we do it? Lots of coffee and pizza. Well, that's partially true. Teamwork ruled the day as editors and reporters dropped other jobs and everyone pitched in.

You have to understand, this story was totally a team effort. That's why the Pulitzer was awarded to the entire staff of the Star-Ledger.

Much of the night was a blur as we pushed to rewrite, re-edit and reconfirm through each of our eight editions. Sometime during that night, I thought of my Morrisville professor Joe Quinn, who had constantly reminded us that the most important part of any story was getting the facts and story right. No second chances!

The day of the Pulitzer announcement, we sent a reporter to The World Room of Columbia University's Journalism building. He informed us we were up for three Pulitzers: the governor's resignation, a feature story and one for international reporting.

When it was announced we had won, the newsroom erupted in handshakes, backslapping and hugs. Champagne was brought out.

My way of celebrating was contacting Journalism Department founder and professor emeritus Jerry Leone. Jerry couldn't have been prouder. I often enjoy reflecting on that phone call.

In the days that followed, editors reminded us that, yes, we had won a Pulitzer, but *only* one.

We still hunger for more.

Jack Durschlag is the lone Pulitzer winner out of three nominees in the 40-year history of the Morrisville College Journalism Department. He is pagination supervisor for the Newark (N.J.) Star-Ledger, where he has worked since 1993. In 1992, he was employed by Forbes Newspapers of Somerville (N.J.) as a copy editor/paginator. He has also worked for the Morristown Daily Record (1986-1992) and the North Jersey Advance newspaper (1986). He currently lives in West Orange, New Jersey with Amy, his wife of nearly 15 years, and has two children, Rachel, 11 and Laryssa, 9.

76

Something Very Special

By Brian McDowell

Assistant Professor of Journalism 1995-Present

There's something very special about this department....

Soon after I started working in public relations at SUNY Morrisville in late July 1985, I met Neal Bandlow and Jerry Leone. I was struck by their passion for 'old-school' journalism—a reporter working hard to find the facts and reporting them without embellishment, always striving to represent the entire story.

Fresh from three years as a general-assignment reporter for the Syracuse Newspapers, I knew the value of gathering facts quickly and transferring those facts—unfiltered—to the printed page. I recall covering the introduction of cruise missiles to Griffiss Air Force Base in Rome, NY, the first U.S. base to receive the strategic missiles. I interviewed the chairman of the Joint Chiefs of Staff that day.

The next day, I walked through a cockroach-infested house in a lower-middle-class neighborhood in Canastota, NY to write a story about the very local, very small health threat.

Humbling is the news business.

Five years into my Morrisville career, I became adjunct instructor of a news writing lab. I looked forward to those two hours each week with such joy; there was something more for me here if I could just reach out and grab it.

So I reached. I asked Jerry if I might ever have a chance to teach in the program. He didn't hesitate. "In spades, Brian," he said. "In *spades*."

I didn't know that my opportunity would come as Jerry departed the program he had built in 1967. But in 1995, he retired—and I entered. Now, as I enter my 13th academic year, I come to work each day with a smile on my face. I have the best job in the world.

This department has always emphasized the basics of good writing and reporting and a tireless dedication to each student. Jerry Leone taught me the importance of family, of tradition, of academic excellence.

.Neal Bandlow taught me that a good professor always includes students in the classroom dialogue—and beyond it. Mary Ellen Mengucci demonstrated the importance of preparing for each and every lecture. They all taught me there is something about this department—something indefinable—that makes it special.

This year, the department introduces two bachelor of science degree programs that will help sustain it through the next 40 years. The degree in Journalism & Communication for Online Media (approved for spring 2008) takes our emphasis on writing onto the Worldwide Web, bringing students into the fastest-growing area of employment in public communication. The degree in Videojournalism will prepare students to produce video packages for broadcast, taking an entrepreneurial approach to the growing world of multimedia.

These programs do not exist anywhere else in higher education at the baccalaureate level. We will build them upon the foundation that was laid 40 years ago by Jerry Leone and Neal Bandlow.

Edward "EJ" Conzola, Gladys Cleland and I still emphasize the basics of public communication and the importance of each student.

EJ has a wealth of real-world experience that enhances every class he teaches. His understanding of the importance 'old-school' journalism plays in today's journalism education makes him a perfect fit for this department.

Gladys Cleland brought with her a great feel for professional broadcasting. Now in her 12th year, she has built a broadcast presence in WCVM Media (she added "Media" to the name a few years ago to reflect the multimedia nature of the production lab) that promises great things in the new bachelor's degree in videojournalism now in the proposal stage.

We all care deeply about linking the 40 years past to the many years to come. And we know that despite all the new technologies and techniques, despite all the changes in journalism education, one thing remains the same.

There's something very special about this department.

Brian L. McDowell earned his B.A. in English at Potsdam State College and his M.A. in Culture & Policy Studies at Empire State College. He started teaching journalism at Morrisville as an adjunct in 1990 and fell in love with the program. In his spare time, he has delighted in serving as 'discount' wedding photographer for several of his former students. He operates Log Cabin Books, *a small publishing company that to date has published this book and five others. He lives in a small log cabin south of Hamilton, NY with his wife, Margaret. Their daughter, Megan (Brian's greatest source of pride), will finish her bachelor's degree in May 2008.*

Editors/Advisors of *The Chimes*

The Chimes has been published continually since 1968 as the official campus newspaper. It is the flagship product of the Journalism department. Former editors-in-chief and their advisors:

1968-69: Grace Cramer   Prof. Leone

1969-70: Cindy Hathaway   Prof. Leone

1970-71: Linda Allison   Prof. Leone

1971-72: Joe DeFrancisco   Prof. Hammond

1972-73: Bill Pedrick   Prof. Hammond

1973-74: Pat "Zonker" Knight   Prof. Reeder

1974-75: Karen Budzynski   Prof. Reeder

1975-76: Loree Martin   Prof. Reeder

1976-77: Justin Mazurowski   Prof. Boulanger

1977-78: Diane Morse   Prof. Boulanger

1978-79: Matt Amodeo   Prof. O'Connor

1979-80: Tony Blanford   Prof. O'Connor

1980-81: Denise Snyder   Prof. Bandlow

1981-82: Elizabeth Cunningham   Prof. Bandlow

1982-83: Gina Carmello/Ruth Stine   Prof. Bandlow

1983-84: Darla Youngs   Prof. Bandlow

1984-85: Val Thorek   Prof. Bandlow

1985-86: Melissa Lanning   Prof. Bandlow

1986-87: Chris Langley   Prof. Bandlow

1987-88: Leslie Brugger/Tim Weldon   Prof. Bandlow

1988-89: Margaret Wagner   Prof. Bandlow

1989-90: Susana Schwartz   Prof. Bandlow

1990-91: Catherine Wilder   Prof. Bandlow

1991-92: Heidi Weber   Prof. Bandlow

1992-93: Maria Hudson   Prof. Bandlow

1993-94: Nicole Reome   Prof. Bandlow

1994-95: Samantha Van Scoy   Prof. Bandlow

1995-96: Andy Goldberger,   Prof. Bandlow
        Katie Haus, Eric Geithner

1996-97: Marilyn "Lynn" Hipp   Prof. Bandlow

1997-98: Jamie Schenk Danielle Manwaring   Prof. Bandlow

1998-99: Terry Bush	Prof. Bandlow
1999-00: Elizabeth "Libby" Parks	Prof. McDowell
2000-01: Robin E. Grant	Prof. McDowell
2001-02: Christine M. Munn	Prof. McDowell
2002-03: Alyson B. Schaefer	Prof. McDowell
2003-04: Blaze K. DiStefano	Prof. McDowell
2004-05: Stephen A. Jensen	Prof. McDowell
2005-06: Marisa J. Bates	Prof. McDowell
2006-07: Brittany Bishop	Prof. McDowell
2007-08: Victoria Gooch	Prof. McDowell

Press Club Scholarship Prize

Since 1976, members of the Journalism faculty honor their top students with the Morrisville Press Club Scholarship Prize. It is the longest ongoing award offered in the program. Honored students:

1976: Gary Maloney, Loree Martin, Al Drowne, Linda Rouse

1977: Anne Rillero, Greg TenEyck, Mark Landauer

1978: Jay Capo, Elaine Sauer, Ann Collea

1979: Bob Myers, Vivian Buisch, Matt Amodeo

1980: Tony Blanford, Carol Shiro, Sonja Fenton

1981: Denise Snyder, Mike Gormley, Mark Emmons, Jim Rogalski

1982: Phyllis Montague, MaryBeth Petterelli, Elizabeth Cunningham

1983: Michelle Germain	**1984:** Darla Youngs
1985: Laura Burch	**1986:** Melissa Lanning
1987: Chris Langley	**1988:** Phyllis Link
1989: Dwayne Bivona	**1990:** Grace Matte
1991: Cathy Wilder	**1992:** Elaine Rutan
1993: Amy Bartholomew	**1994:** Karen Sheldon
1995: Shawn Kime	**1996** Yoshi Shinya
1997: Stephanie Youngers	**1998:** Matthew Burns
1999: Sandra Fish, Theresa Bush	
2000: Lynda Janovsky	**2001:** Amelia Vecsernyes
2002: Christine Munn	**2003:** Stephanie Barish
2004: Tisha Overend	**2005:** Stephen Jensen
2006 Marissa Bates	**2007:** Jawann Haynes

Morrisville Journalism Department 40th Reunion—July 21, 2007